magpie

Sweets and Savories from Philadelphia's Favorite Pie Boutique

HOLLY RICCIARDI

with

MIRIAM HARRIS

RUNNING PRESS
PHILADELPHIA · LONDON

Published by Running Press,
A Member of the Perseus Books Group

Printed in China

Books published by Running Press are available at special discounts for bulk purchases in the
United States by corporations, institutions, and other organizations. For more information,
please contact the Special Markets Department at the Perseus Books Group, 2300 Chestnut
Street, Suite 200, Philadelphia, PA 19103, or call (800) 810-4145, ext. 5000, or e-mail
special.markets@perseusbooks.com.

ISBN 978-0-7624-5453-2
Library of Congress Control Number: 2015937006
E-book ISBN 978-0-7624-5805-9

9   8   7   6   5   4   3   2   1
Digit on the right indicates the number of this printing

Designed by Susan Van Horn
Edited by Kristen Green Wiewora
Prop styling by Carrie Purcell
Food styling by Carrie Purcell and Holly Ricciardi
Typography: Archer, Hera Big, and Brandon Text

Running Press Book Publishers
2300 Chestnut Street
Philadelphia, PA 19103-4371

Visit us on the web!
www.offthemenublog.com

To Greg, for ignoring the
possibilities of the fool in me
and for believing in the
possibilities of greatness in me.

contents

introduction

I flipped the sign in Magpie's storefront window to "Open" for the very first time on September 1, 2012. It was a characteristically steamy, late-summer Philadelphia morning. And it was perfect.

Perfect timing for the opening day of a season-centric pie shop: smack-dab on the cusp between summer and fall, that amazing moment just before the lush summer tide of berries and stone fruits recedes, when the most flavorful corn and tomatoes are still abundant, and yet the first wave of early-variety fall apples is already sweeping in.

Reading through that opening-day menu is like watching a movie-camera slow-pan shot of a long banquet table laid out with an all-pie, end-of-summer extravaganza.

But that final blush of summer was going, going, gone, and by October 1, fall was upon us, and we had a completely different menu. Just one fruit pie remained the same, the Caramel Apple (page 46), in a new lineup of sweet pies that included Coffee-Choc-olate-Cinnamon Pecan (page 179) and Pear Ginger Oatmeal Crumb (page 56), along with our year-round signature pie, Butterscotch Bourbon (page 160). Savory-wise, the Tomato Cheddar Corn Pie (page 204) was a distant memory. In its place: Smoked Gouda Butternut Squash Pie (page 215) and Mole Chili Frito Potpies (page 237).

All within our first month of business—how crazy is that? What kind of lunatic opens a restaurant with full knowledge that the menu will have to be overhauled on a monthly basis—sometimes even more frequently

(hello and goodbye, sour cherries!)—to keep pace with the ebb and flow of fresh, local, seasonal produce?

Well, I was born and raised in a small town in the south-central Pennsylvania countryside. Pare away a few layers of trendy jargon, shrug off the food-fetishism, and what's nowadays touted as locavorian, seasonal, farm-to-table cuisine bears strong resemblance to the way my family back home has been provisioning, cooking, and eating for generations. (This is not the place to get into it, but as far as nouvelle nose-to-tail cuisine is concerned, I've got just one word for you: scrapple!)

Back there in Carlisle, my hometown, extended family literally extended in all directions. Living within blocks of one another were my grandparents, great-aunts, uncles, and lots of cousins. Even my great-grandparents lived two blocks away. The house I grew up in was catty-corner to my grandparents' backyard, which had a grove of fruit trees and a big kitchen garden. In town, my grandfather owned and ran a grocery and butcher shop while, for decades, my great-grandmother sold her famous pies and cakes at the Carlisle Country Market.

So, yes, to go along with my country upbringing I've inherited some serious baking genes. My mother, at an early age, took on the self-appointed role of baking protégé to her grandmother. Mom grew up into a formidable baker—even raising five children and work-

like apple dumplings, whoopie pies, and shoofly pie (page 176). No treat was ever store-bought—not the caramel popcorn balls doled out at Halloween, not the peanut butter eggs at Easter, and certainly not the two dozen different kinds of cookies at Christmas.

And the holiday feasts! In my family, the dessert lineup is always in equal proportion to savories. (Take a moment to picture that: a great big turkey/ham/roast, plus a dozen or so traditional sides—all matched pound for pound by a parade of pies and other treats.) When I was a kid, my grandparents shared the holiday cooking, with my grandfather (being a butcher) preparing the meats and my grandmother making the side dishes (her candied sweet potatoes, which could double as dessert, are an inspiration for my Roasted Sweet Potato Pie, page 142),

To me, there is no other food that celebrates the season— the here-and-now—like pie does, and no other food that makes us feel the way pie does: loved.

ing full-time as an overnight switchboard operator at the local hospital, she made everything herself. No exaggeration: in addition to home cooking all of our meals, my mother made any and all sweets herself. She didn't serve dessert after dinner every night, but she routinely baked whatever suited the season, anything that was in harvest or struck her fancy. In addition to typical Americana sweets like sugar cookies, oatmeal cookies, zucchini bread, banana bread, and fruit crisps and pies, there were the south-central Pennsy staples

and my mother focused primarily on the dessert spread. These days, my mother has taken full charge of holiday meals. She has four daughters helping out (to the extent she allows), and the dessert menu maintains its spectacular proportions.

Getting back to the "what was I thinking" question, here's the best answer I can muster: In a world where well-made sweet treats of all sorts have become pretty easy to come by, great pie remains a rarity. Pie-making has become a nearly lost art. To me, there

is no other food that celebrates the season—the here-and-now—like pie does, and no other food that makes us feel the way pie does: loved. That's what I seek to serve up at Magpie, one slice at a time.

I've divvied up everything you need to know into four chapters, starting with dough because that's where any good pie begins. Then come the most seasonally driven recipes: Fruity Pies. Next up are the (Mostly) Creamy Pies. Then, because pie isn't always just for dessert, there's a selection of Quiches, Potpies, and Other Savories. Throughout, I've included sidebars and supplemental how-tos to help with the handicraft. Many of the recipes come with an alternative "spin."

Pie is, for the most part, slow food. I hope you can settle in and take your sweet time, taking as much pleasure and pride in the process of pie-making as you do in the end product. Well, almost as much, anyway.

Enjoy—and happy pie-baking!

flaky piecrust

AM NOT GOING TO BE SHY ABOUT COMING RIGHT OUT AND SAYING IT—OURS IS A PIE DOUGH OF TRUE GREATNESS.

It produces a piecrust that is delectably flaky, tender to the bite, and sturdy as all get-out. The dough keeps wonderfully, whether it languishes for several days in the fridge, goes straight in the freezer in its initial disk form, or gets frozen after it's been chilled and rolled out into a sheet (or even fitted into a pan). What's more, it's phenomenally versatile. We use it for all manner of sweet pie—from airy mousse to lush fruit; from single, double, and latticed to mini pies and hand pies. And we use the very same dough for each and every one of our savory pies, potpies, and quiches.

The magic of the recipe is in the perfect equilibrium of its six humble ingredients: all-purpose white flour with the right level of protein; sufficient fat, in the form of a spot-on ratio of unsalted butter to vegetable shortening (both frozen); small, flavor-enhancing measures of granulated sugar and salt; and just barely enough ice-cold water to persuade the mixture to cohere.

Then there's our mixing method, which is a hybrid approach I've developed in the course of turning out thousands upon thousands of handmade pies. In my experience, this method is unbeatable. You start out using a food processor to swirl together the flour, salt, and sugar, then quickly cut in first the butter and then the shortening. Then you switch to hand mixing: Dump the flour-and-fat mixture into a big bowl, and use a curved bowl scraper to fold in the water, just until clumps begin to form. All told, the process takes maybe 5 minutes. You have something that barely looks like dough when you first pat it together and wrap it up. Into the fridge it goes, and the next day it emerges, smooth and lovely and ready to be rolled, panned, and baked to flaky perfection.

·····⤙ DON'T FEAR THE PIECRUST ⤚·····

Despite everything you may have heard and any pie-baking angst you may have experienced in the past, great piecrust really and truly is not difficult to make. And it doesn't require any fancy ingredients.

What making great piecrust does require, first and foremost, is *care*, as in gathering a few basic components, measuring them accurately, and combining them properly. There's some basic handiwork involved—rolling and panning your bottom crust takes a light touch and a little practice, and there's some know-how you'll need to properly handle a crust that has to be prebaked. But if you start out with a good, clear set of instructions, an uncluttered workspace, an open, pie-loving heart, and a reasonable set of aesthetic expectations, plus a few Magpie trade secrets, you'll get the hang of it.

Just as important as all the hands-on techniques is the hands-off time. Dough must have the alone time it needs. Always, always, always chill your dough overnight—as in a full 8 hours or more—before you roll it out!

Making great piecrust does take time, but nearly all of that time is for the dough to rest or bake. Actual hands-on, active time adds up to a grand total of maybe 60 minutes at most, and much less than that once you learn a few basic moves.

······⤙⤚ INGREDIENT ESSENTIALS ⤙⤚······
Here's what you'll need:

All-purpose white flour with 10% to 11% protein content, which means Pillsbury or Gold Medal (10.5% protein) are good choices. Bleached or unbleached is fine.

Granulated sugar and fine salt—any brand at all.

Unsalted butter with 23% to 24% fat content. Regional brands are often a good way to go; I've always used Land O'Lakes, which I grew up with because some of their farms are in my hometown of Carlisle, Pennsylvania. Decades later, they still stock the dairy cases of supermarkets in the Philly area.

Vegetable shortening. Yes: a bit of this is essential to a flaky-yet-sturdy crust because it has a higher melting point than butter, so it holds up as the crust bakes and lends structure that produces nice strong flakes. (If you have a good source of very high-quality leaf lard, you could experiment with substituting that for the shortening, but we use Crisco at the shop.) Because the shortening needs to be in small cubes for the pie dough, my advice is to buy in sticks rather than by the tub—much easier to freeze and dice.

PIE DOUGH TOOLS

Digital kitchen scale: A must-have for making good pie dough. These days, a very good digital scale can be had for under $20—worth every penny.

Bench scraper: Ideal for cubing butter and shortening; also very useful for coaxing the edge of thinly rolled (and highly stretch-prone) dough off the work surface.

Food processor: Hands-down, so to speak, the best and speediest tool for the all-important job of cutting together flour and fat.

Curved plastic bowl scraper: For mixing the water into the dough, nothing beats this ultra-cheap little implement. Find one for a few bucks at any store that sells kitchen supplies. Make sure you get one made of stiff plastic (not rubbery silicone).

Rolling pin: Every baker has his or her own preferred rolling implement. My personal favorite is a 20-inch, no-handled, untapered plastic pin that's meant for rolling fondant. My mom swears by a sturdy old vintage model, complete with handles and ball bearings. Some bakers insist that a tapered French pin is where it's at; others are all about untapered wooden dowel. Whatever you are most comfortable with is just fine.

Long metal ruler or straightedge: From measuring various size dough rounds to cutting lattice strips, the 18-inch, stainless-steel ruler in the kitchen at the shop is in constant use.

Pie pans: Keep two standard 9-inch (23-cm) pans on hand (9 inches is the width of the top; the sides should be sloped and 1 to 1½ inches [3 to 4 cm] deep at most), either metal or oven-safe glass. No need to get fancy; decent standard brands are just fine. Don't use disposable foil pans; they are not properly sized for 9-inch (23-cm) pies, so they won't accommodate the recipes in this book. Ceramic pie pans are nice, but be sure to check the size—most are for deep-dish pies, a larger volume than a standard 9-inch (23-cm) pie.

Standard 12-cup metal muffin pan: For mini pies.

One (9-inch / 23-cm) springform pan: For quiche.

Eight (4½ x 2-inch / 11 x 5-cm) mini springform pans: For potpies; these pans are easy to find online, in the baking section of many craft stores, and at various chain stores carrying specialty cookware. (Alternative: 4½ x 2-inch / 11 x 5-cm ring molds.)

Baking sheets: You'll need two large, rimmed baking sheets—called half-sheet pans at restaurant supply stores (18 x 13 inches / 46 x 33 cm). Jellyroll pans (17 x 11 inches / 43 x 28 cm) will work, too. They're essential for getting pies in and out of the oven without sloshing the filling or mangling the crust. Baking on a sheet also catches fat that cooks out of the crust, as well as any filling that may boil over.

Parchment paper: For lining baking sheets (making for easy clean-up) and lining pie shells during the prebake.

Dried beans (a.k.a. pie weights): At Magpie we keep a 10-gallon tub of dried black turtle beans in the corner of the kitchen—that's about 40 pounds. You'll need about 2 pounds (4 cups) of beans to fill a 9-inch piecrust; at least double that much for a quiche or eight individual potpies. Once beans have been used as pie weights, they can't be cooked and eaten, but they can continue to serve as pie weights for quite a long time—until they start shedding their skins. We reuse ours 3 to 4 times a week and replace once or twice a year.

Extra Gear

(handy, but entirely optional)

Plastic or silicone rolling mat: Marked with circles of various circumferences, a mat provides a very useful guide for rolling out your dough. Plus it doesn't grab ahold of dough like a countertop does, so it requires less flour.

Pastry cutter: Like a teeny pizza cutter, this tool is nice for cutting dough into strips for lattice or shapes, though you can certainly get the job done quite well with a pizza cutter or regular kitchen knife (strips) or a paring knife or cookie cutter (shapes).

Pizza stone: Park it on the middle rack in your oven, and set your baking sheets/pie pans right on it; it will help brown up the bottom of the crust and hold the temperature of your oven better.

·····⋈⊲ METHOD FUNDAMENTALS ⊳⋈·····
A few non-negotiables:

Weigh out your ingredients. Yes indeed, use a kitchen scale and weigh each of those six ingredients you put into your piecrust. Why? Because it is an inescapable fact that volume measures are altered by humidity and other factors. The amount of flour, for instance, that fits in a measuring cup is different from one day to the next.

Bottom line: Good piecrust is all about preserving precise ratios between the ingredients, and weighing them is the only way to achieve this. Plus, the time and effort of weighing is minimal—arguably easier and less messy than using measuring cups and spoons. So just do it! The results will delight you.

Have your butter and vegetable shortening cubed and frozen before you start. (Note: the shortening won't freeze hard, but it will firm up, which makes it much easier to cut into small pieces and keep from globbing back together.)

Put your water on ice. On dough-making days at Magpie, we keep a pitcher of ice water in the kitchen and pour through a little strainer to portion the water out for each batch of dough. I recommend you do the same.

Keep the butter, shortening, and water cold. If you get interrupted, even briefly, put everything in the refrigerator until you can get back to focusing on your pie dough.

Plan to bake your pie at least one day after you make the pie dough—it needs a full night's rest before it is ready to roll. (This is crucial to having dough that is workable and bakes up into a crust that is not only tender and flaky, but also keeps its shape and doesn't shrink or otherwise misbehave.)

magpie dough for flaky piecrust

There are three distinct, fundamental steps here: 1) weigh, 2) mix, and 3) chill. Once you've chilled your dough overnight, you can proceed with rolling, panning, prebaking (if needed), and finishing your pie.

MAKES ENOUGH DOUGH FOR ANY OF THE FOLLOWING:

2 (9-inch / 23-cm) **single-crust pies,**

1 (9-inch / 23-cm) **double-crust or lattice-top pie,**

8 (4 x 2-inch / 10 x 5-cm) **potpies,**

12 (2 x 1-inch / 5 x 3-cm) **mini pies,**

1 (9 x 3-inch / 23 x 8-cm) **quiche, or**

8 (4-inch / 10-cm) **hand pies (plus trimmings)**

1) Weigh

312 grams / 2½ cups
all-purpose flour

28 grams / 2 tablespoons
granulated sugar

6 grams / 1 teaspoon fine salt

170 grams / ¾ cup cold unsalted
butter, cut into ¼-inch cubes
and frozen

60 grams / ¼ cup vegetable
shortening, preferably in baking
stick form, frozen, cut into ¼-inch
pieces, and put back in the freezer

130 grams / ½ cup + 1 tablespoon
ice-cold water

2) Mix

Combine the flour, sugar, and salt in the bowl of a food processor and pulse the machine 3 times to blend. Scatter the frozen butter cubes over the flour mixture. Pulse the machine 5 to 7 times, holding each pulse for 5 full seconds, to cut all of the butter into pea-size pieces. Scatter the pieces of frozen shortening over the flour-and-butter mixture. Pulse the machine 4 more 1-second pulses to blend the shortening with the flour. The mixture will resemble coarse cornmeal, but will be a bit more floury and riddled with pale butter bits (no pure-white shortening should be visible; see figure 1, next page).

Turn the mixture out into a large mixing bowl, and make a small well in the center. If you find a few butter clumps that are closer to marble size than pea size (about ¼ inch in diameter), carefully pick them out and give them a quick smoosh with your fingers. Pour the cold water into the well (fig. 2, next page). Use a curved bowl scraper to lightly scoop the flour mixture up

(Continued)

17

and over the water, covering the water to help get the absorption started. Continue mixing by scraping the flour up from the sides and bottom of the bowl into the center, rotating the bowl as you mix (fig. 4), and occasionally pausing to clean off the scraper with your finger or the side of the bowl, until the mixture begins to gather into clumps but is still very crumbly (fig. 5). (If you are working in very dry conditions and the ingredients remain very floury and refuse to clump together at this stage, add another tablespoon of ice-cold water.)

Lightly gather the clumps with your fingers and use your palm to fold over and press the dough a few times (figs. 6–7; don't knead!—just give the dough a few quick squishes), until it just begins to come together into a single large mass. It will be a raggedy wad (fig. 8), moist but not damp, that barely holds together; this is exactly as it should be—all it needs is a good night's rest in the fridge.

For single- and double-crust pies, mini pies, potpies, or hand pies: Divide the dough into 2 equal portions, gently shape each portion into a flat disk 1½ to 2 inches thick, and wrap each tightly with plastic wrap.

For quiche, leave the dough in one piece, flatten it into a single large disk 1½ to 2 inches thick (fig. 9), and wrap tightly with plastic wrap.

3) Chill

No ifs, ands, or buts, the dough must have its beauty sleep. That means 8 hours in the refrigerator at the very least. Extra rest is just fine; feel free to let the wrapped dough sit in the fridge for up to 3 days before rolling. (The dough may discolor slightly. No worries. This is merely oxidization and will not affect the flavor or appearance of your finished piecrust.)

Note: At this stage, the wrapped dough can be put in a freezer bag and frozen for up to 2 months. Defrost overnight in the refrigerator before rolling.

TO MIX WITH A PASTRY BLENDER

You can use a pastry blender if you don't have a food processor. Working quickly to prevent the butter from warming and softening, use a whisk to combine the dry ingredients in a large bowl. Scatter on the butter, and cut it into the flour with a pastry blender until all of the butter bits are pea-sized. Scatter on the shortening, and cut it into the butter and flour mixture until the only visible lumps are butter (which will remain firm while the vegetable shortening warms and softens almost immediately).

Make a small well in the center of the mixture, and proceed with the recipe as written.

single-crust pie shell

The dough recipe (page 17) makes enough for two single-crust shells. To save yourself some time next time around, you can repeat the process outlined below to make a second panned and fluted crust to freeze (double-wrapped in plastic). This is a perfect way to be prepared for coming across a great sale on fresh fruit, or to make a nice dessert to take to a party the next day.

MAKES 1 (9-inch / 23-cm) PIECRUST

½ recipe Magpie Dough for Flaky Piecrust (page 17), chilled overnight

1) Roll

Lightly flour a smooth work surface and a rolling pin.

Take a chilled disk of dough out of the fridge. Give it a couple of firm squeezes just to say hello, then unwrap it and set it on the floured work surface.

Set the pin crosswise on the dough and press down firmly, making a nice deep channel across the full width of the disk (fig. 1). Turn the disk 180 degrees and repeat, making a second indentation, forming a plus sign (fig. 2).

Use your rolling pin to press down each of the wedges, turning the dough 45 degrees each time. This will give you the beginnings of a thick circle (fig. 3).

Now, rolling from the center outward and rotating the dough a quarter turn to maintain a circular shape, roll the dough out to a 13-inch circle with an even thickness of ¼ inch (figs. 4–9; see Tips for Dough-Friendly Rolling, page 28).

(Continued)

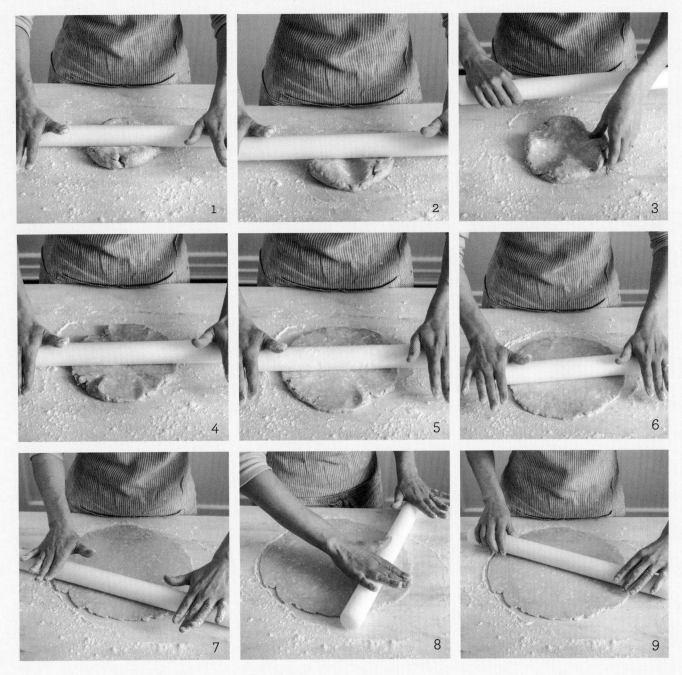

2) Pan

Set your 9-inch (23-cm) pie pan alongside the circle of dough. Brush off any loose flour, carefully fold the dough circle in half, transfer it to the pan, and unfold (figs. 1–3).

At this point the dough will be lying across rather than fitted into the pan. Now, without stretching the dough, set the dough down into the pan so that it is flush up against the sides and bottom. The best way to do this is to gingerly lift the dough and gently shift it around so that it settles into the pan bit by bit. Use a very light touch to help cozy it in (figs. 4–6).

To flute the edge, fold the overhang under to form a 1-inch wall that rests on the lip of the pan with the seam slightly below the pan's top edge (figs. 7–8). Go around the edge of the pan and use a very light touch to firm up the wall to an even thickness from the bottom to the top and all the way around (fig. 9). Flute the edge of the crust at about 1-inch intervals, pressing from the inside with the knuckle of your index finger while supporting on the outside with the thumb and index finger of your opposite hand (figs. 10–12). Don't pinch the dough, you want the flute to look like a thick rope.

Transfer the crust to the refrigerator to chill while you make your filling or to the freezer to prepare it for prebaking (see the next page). Alternatively, at this point the crust can be covered tightly in plastic wrap and refrigerated for up to 3 days or double-wrapped and frozen for up to 2 months (defrost overnight in the refrigerator before filling and baking or prebaking, or at room temperature for 30 minutes).

(Continued)

10

11

12

3) **Prebake**

To prebake the shell, chill the panned, fluted piecrust in the freezer until firm, 15 to 20 minutes.

Preheat the oven to 375°F (190°C) with a rack in the center. Line a rimmed baking sheet with parchment paper. Cut an additional 13 x 13-inch square of parchment.

Set the pan on the lined baking sheet. Set the square of parchment in the pie shell and gently smooth it into place, pleating as needed to fit it up against the bottom and sides of the shell. The edges of the paper will project beyond the rim of the pan; just leave them standing straight up.

Fill the shell to the top with dried beans. Gently stir the beans around with your fingers to ensure that there are no air pockets (especially down in the corners where the sides and bottom of the pan meet). Top up with more beans as needed to come level with the top of the fluted edge of the piecrust.

Slide the baking sheet into the oven and bake the shell for 25 minutes.

Set out a wire rack and, alongside it, a mixing bowl. Take the baking sheet out of the oven and set it on the rack; bring together the points of the parchment (which won't be hot to the touch), and carefully lift out the beans and transfer them to the bowl.

Slide the baking sheet back into the oven and bake the crust another 7 minutes (or until pale golden) for prebaked, or 10 minutes (until golden brown) for fully prebaked, depending on your recipe's requirements. Cool on a wire rack.

double-crust pie shell

My mother would use the sugary cinnamon goo from her apple filling to help seal the top and bottom crusts of her apple pies together. She said the crust's edge (her favorite part) is even better with that swirl of cinnamon inside. We use this technique for all of our double-crust fruit pies.

Though they need no further embellishment to be a thing of beauty, adding cutouts is an easy way to have fun with double-crust pies. You can get creative with venting the top crust by cutting pretty little shapes and patterns. Or you can use scrap dough to make little appliqués—cutouts from scrap dough that you attach to the top crust just before baking.

MAKES 1 (9-inch / 23-cm) DOUBLE-CRUST PIE SHELL

1 recipe Magpie Dough for Flaky Piecrust (page 17), chilled overnight

Retrieve one disk of dough from the refrigerator. Roll and pan the bottom crust as directed for Single-Crust Pie Shell, pages 20–23, but don't fold or flute the edge; just trim the overhang (if needed) to 1 inch all the way around. Cover the bottom crust with plastic wrap and put the pan in the refrigerator while you roll the dough for the top shell.

Fetch the second disk of dough from the refrigerator and roll it out as directed for Single-Crust Pie Shell, page 20. Fold the circle of dough in half, carefully transfer it to a parchment-lined baking sheet, and unfold to lay flat. Slide the baking sheet into the refrigerator.

Once your bottom crust is filled as directed for the pie you're making, pull the baking sheet out of the fridge, cut decorative vent holes in the top crust if you like, then fold it in half and carefully lift it onto the top of the pie. Unfold the dough, center it on the pie (fig. 1), and trim the edge to a 1-inch overhang all the way around.

Pinch the two edges of dough together, roll outward and under to form a ledge, and tuck the edge inside the lip of the pie pan (figs. 2–6). Crimp the edge all the way around or flute as directed for single crust (page 23).

If you have not already cut decorative vent holes, use kitchen shears or a small, sharp knife to cut 4 slits, each about 2 inches long, near the center of the top crust.

Follow your pie recipe instructions for glazing, sprinkling with sugar, and baking.

TIPS FOR DOUGH-FRIENDLY ROLLING

For a piecrust that's tender and flaky and holds its shape while it bakes, it's essential to roll the dough all the way out to the full breadth and thickness needed without stretching it.

Always roll from the center of the circle outward—not up and down the full length or across the full width of the dough (doing so will get you a non-circle of uneven thickness).

Take care to use the pin in a rolling motion that squeezes the dough outward into a larger circle. (I've taught hundreds of pie-making classes and found that many people, without realizing it, push the pin across the dough without really rolling it and thus pull and stretch the heck out of the poor dough. This is right up there with the top causes of piecrust trouble).

Roll with medium-firm pressure, releasing as you reach the edge (this will help maintain an even thickness and prevent stretching the dough at the outer edges).

Keep the dough moving. Rotating the dough on your work surface as you roll it helps prevent sticking and keeps the dough relaxed.

Be vigilant about not letting your dough stick to the counter. When you turn the dough, be on the lookout for sticky spots beginning to form and sprinkle a little bit of flour underneath the dough as needed.

Use no more flour than needed to keep the dough from sticking; adding significant amounts of flour to the dough can make it dry and bitter tasting.

If your dough warms up too much while you are rolling and starts to feel soft and wet, don't fret—but don't keep working it, either. Slide it onto a baking sheet, cover with plastic wrap, and put it in the fridge for about 15 to 20 minutes to rest, chill down, and firm up.

When rolling, take a moment now and then to measure the diameter and thickness of your dough so you know for sure when you are getting close and so you don't roll the dough out too thin.

If you have time, carefully transfer the folded, rolled-out dough onto a parchment-lined baking sheet; unfold the sheet to lay flat and slide the sheet into the refrigerator to give the dough another rest (15 to 20 minutes) before proceeding with panning or cutting.

lattice-top pie shell

Depending upon the type of pie we're making, we use two types of lattice. One is woven from ten 1-inch-wide strips of dough for a traditional-style pie top. For a more contemporary look, we cut fewer strips but make them double-width. Brushed with egg wash and baked, both styles emerge golden, puffed, and lovely. Sprinkle coarse sugar on top before baking to give your lattice pies some sparkle.

MAKES 1 (9-inch / 23-cm) LATTICE-TOP PIE SHELL

1 recipe Magpie Dough for Flaky Piecrust (page 17), chilled overnight

Retrieve one disk of dough from the refrigerator. Roll and pan the bottom crust as directed for a Single-Crust Pie Shell (pages 20–23), but don't proceed with forming the wall of dough and fluting the edge; just trim the overhang (if needed) to 1 inch all the way around. Cover the bottom crust with plastic wrap and put the pan in the refrigerator while you roll the dough for the top shell.

For a traditional lattice top, fetch the second disk of dough from the refrigerator and roll it out as directed for a Single-Crust Pie Shell (page 20). Fold the circle of dough in half and carefully transfer it to a parchment-lined baking sheet, then unfold to lay flat. Use a pizza cutter, pastry wheel, or large knife, along with a ruler or straightedge, to cut the dough into ten 1-inch-wide strips. Cover them with plastic wrap, slide the baking sheet into the refrigerator, and chill the strips until the pie is ready to be topped.

Once your bottom crust is filled as directed for the pie you're making, pull the baking sheet out of the fridge and lay 5 of the strips vertically across the filling, spacing evenly (fig. 1, next page). Fold back every other strip halfway and add a dough strip perpendicular to the first layer of lattice strips so that it crosses the unfolded strips that are lying flat (fig. 2, next page). Swap the folded and unfolded vertical strips, folding the other half of the strips back over the first horizontal strip, and adding a second

(Continued)

29

├ *traditional lattice* ┤

horizontal dough strip across the flat strips (figs. 3–4). Repeat the process to lattice the rest of the pie. Pinch the two edges of dough together, roll outward and under to form a ledge, and tuck the edge inside the lip of the pie pan (figs. 2–6, page 27). Crimp the edge all the way around. Follow your pie recipe instructions for sprinkling with sugar and baking.

For a wide-strip lattice top, follow the directions for the traditional lattice, but cut the dough into six 2-inch-wide strips, and begin weaving the lattice by laying 3 of the strips vertically across the filling. Fold back the two outer strips halfway and add a dough strip horizontally across the center of the pie so that it crosses the flat strip. Swap the folded and unfolded vertical strips and add a second horizontal strip across the flat strips (fig. 1). Repeat once more with the remaining strip to complete the lattice (figs. 2–3). To finish the edge, follow the directions for the traditional lattice, above. Follow your pie recipe instructions for glazing, sprinkling with sugar, and baking.

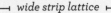

wide strip lattice

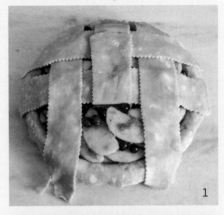

1

2

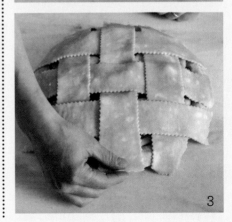

3

SCRAP DOUGH: WASTE NOT, WANT NOT

Scrap dough, those bits and bobs trimmed off the edges of your top crust and left behind on the counter after you've cut out the rounds for your mini pies or potpies, is not something to be discarded. No way! Scrap dough is worthy of being gathered up and saved—prized, even. If you handle your dough trimmings gently—don't knead or squish into a ball, just pile 'em up in a freeform stack, wrap 'em up, and leave 'em be in the fridge or freezer—you will be rewarded with puff-pastry-like flakiness that surpasses even your most carefully crafted piecrust. Great ways to up-cycle your scrap dough include: Pie "Fries" (page 34), decorative tops for mini pies (page 32), or a quick batch of hand pies (page 40).

shells for mini pies

For each mini pie shell, make sure the dough is pressed up to the top of the muffin cup. Chilling before baking helps prevent the dough from sliding down in the cup.

◆ MAKES 12 (2-inch / 5-cm) MINI PIECRUSTS ◆

1 recipe Magpie Dough for
Flaky Piecrust (page 17),
chilled overnight

Retrieve one disk of dough from the refrigerator and roll as directed for a Single-Crust Pie Shell (page 20). Use a 4-inch cutter (or, like we do in the shop, use an empty coffee can with an opening that diameter) to cut the dough into six 4-inch rounds. Transfer the rounds to a parchment-lined baking sheet and set the sheet in the refrigerator. Gather up the scraps, wrap them in plastic, and keep in the refrigerator for another use (see Scrap Dough, page 31). Repeat the process with the second disk of dough, adding six more rounds to the baking sheet and the additional trimmings to the scrap dough.

Fit the twelve circles of dough into the cups of a standard muffin pan, pleating as needed and pressing lightly to snug the dough up against the bottom and sides of each cup. (If the dough starts to feel soft and moist, set the muffin pan in the refrigerator and let the dough firm back up.) Don't fuss much with the dough—these crusts are meant to have an adorably rustic look—just keep the dough level with or slightly above the rim of the baking cup. Cover with plastic wrap and slide the tin into the refrigerator until you are ready to proceed with filling or prebaking the shells.

To prebake: Freeze the crusts 15 to 20 minutes or until firm.

Preheat the oven to 375°F (190°C) with a rack in the center.

Cut twelve 5 x 5-inch squares of parchment paper or aluminum foil. Line the shells with the parchment squares, gently smoothing and pleating the

paper into place up against the bottom and sides of each crust and leaving the corners of the paper standing straight up. Fill each shell to the rim with beans, stirring with a finger to settle the beans and topping up as needed.

Slide the muffin tin into the oven and bake the shells 20 minutes. While the shells are baking, set out a wire rack and, alongside it, a mixing bowl.

Set the pan on the wire rack and let the shells cool for 10 minutes, then carefully gather the corners of each parchment square together to lift out the beans and transfer them to the bowl. Slide the muffin tin back into the oven and bake the shells another 5 minutes, or until lightly browned (see photo on page 205).

PIE "FRIES"

You can use fresh pie dough to make these tasty treats, but the flakiest pie fries are made with leftover dough trimmings (see Scrap Dough, page 31). When gathering up your scrap dough, make sure you press the pieces together gently—do not knead the dough. Wrap the piled-up dough scraps in plastic wrap and chill until firm before rolling. How big a batch you make depends entirely upon on how much scrap dough you have accumulated. (It keeps brilliantly in the freezer: just be sure to tuck the wrapped dough into a freezer bag. Defrost overnight in the fridge.) At the shop, we serve these as an accompaniment to ice cream, hot chocolate, and espresso drinks.

MAKES A DOZEN OR MORE "FRIES"

Chilled pie dough scraps

1 large egg yolk

Coarse raw sugar or sanding sugar, for sprinkling

Flaky sea salt or kosher salt, for sprinkling

Preheat the oven to 375°F (190°C) with a rack in the center. Line a baking sheet with parchment paper.

Lightly flour a smooth work surface and roll the chilled dough out into a ¼-inch-thick rectangle. With one of the long sides of the rectangle facing you, use a pastry wheel or sharp knife to cut the dough into long, 1-inch-wide strips, then cut each long strip in half crosswise. Transfer the strips to the parchment-lined baking sheet, spacing them 1 inch apart.

Whisk the egg yolk with 1 tablespoon water. Lightly brush the strips with the egg wash and sprinkle them with sugar and a couple pinches of salt.

Slide the baking sheet into the oven and bake the fries 12 to 15 minutes, until golden brown and puffed. Keep an eye on them; they go from golden to burnt very quickly.

Let cool slightly—eating them warm is the BEST!

potpie shells

Potpie-making becomes a less time-consuming proposition if you bake the shells in advance and freeze them. They keep well for a month when wrapped, and you'll be set to whip up a batch whenever the mood strikes or cold weather blows in. Thaw frozen shells at room temperature, then refresh them in a 350°F (175°C) oven for 5 to 7 minutes before filling.

◆ **MAKES 8** (4 x 2-inch / 10 x 5-cm) **SHELLS** ◆

1 recipe Magpie Dough for Flaky Piecrust (page 17), chilled overnight

Divide each disk of chilled dough into four equal portions; flatten each portion into a disk, then roll out into eight 7-inch circles that are ¼ inch thick (see Tips for Dough-Friendly Rolling, page 28). Set the rounds on a parchment-lined baking sheet and chill 30 minutes before panning.

Fit each chilled 7-inch circle of dough into a 4½ x 2-inch (11 x 5-cm) spring-form pan, pleating here and there as needed to fit and pressing lightly to snug the dough up against the bottom and sides of the pan. If there is any overhanging dough, simply fold it in, making sure the top edge is even all around (see photo on page 33).

Chill the panned dough in the freezer until firm, 15 to 20 minutes.

Preheat the oven to 375°F (190°C) with a rack in the center. Line a baking sheet with parchment paper. Cut eight 8-inch squares of aluminum foil or parchment paper.

Line the shells with the foil squares, gently smoothing and pleating the foil into place up close against the bottom and sides of each crust and leaving the corners of the foil standing straight up. Fill each shell to the rim of the crust with beans, stirring with a finger to settle the beans and topping up as needed.

Set the pans on the parchment-lined baking sheet. Slide the sheet into the oven and bake the shells 30 minutes, rotating halfway through the baking time.

Set the sheet on a wire rack and let the shells cool all the way to room temperature before carefully gathering the corners of each foil square together to lift out the beans.

WHY PREBAKE?

Prebaking—also known as blind baking—is used for two types of pies: those with no-bake fillings (such as mousse), and those with fillings that do get baked but at low temperatures that aren't sufficient to fully bake the crust (lemon curd, for example, and all Magpie quiches). Weights are needed to hold the panned shell in place and prevent the crust from shrinking while it bakes. The Magpie way: Line with parchment or foil and fill to the brim with dried beans.

quiche shell

It's the very same dough as our other piecrusts, but baking our quiche shell in a tall springform rather than a regular pie pan endows it with statuesque proportions.

MAKES 1 (9 x 3-inch / 23 x 8-cm) **SHELL**

1 recipe Magpie Dough for Flaky Piecrust (page 17), kept as single large disk and chilled overnight

Lightly flour a smooth work surface and rolling pin. Line a large baking sheet with parchment paper.

Take the chilled disk of dough out of the refrigerator. Give it a couple of firm squeezes just to say hello, then unwrap it and set it on the floured work surface.

Set the pin crosswise on the dough and press down firmly, making a nice deep channel across the full width of the disk (fig. 1, page 21). Turn the disk 180 degrees and repeat, making a second indentation, forming a plus sign (fig. 2, page 21).

Use your rolling pin to press down each of the wedges, turning the dough 45 degrees each time. This will give you the beginnings of a thick circle (fig. 3, page 21).

Now, rolling from the center outward and rotating the dough a quarter turn to maintain a circular shape, roll the dough out to a 15-inch circle with an even thickness of ¼ inch (figs 4–9; see also Tips for Dough-Friendly Rolling, page 28).

Brush off any loose flour. Fold the circle in half, carefully transfer it to the parchment-lined baking sheet, then unfold, cover with plastic wrap, and chill at least 30 minutes before panning.

Set your 9-inch (23-cm) springform pan alongside the 15-inch dough circle. Carefully fold the circle in half, transfer it to the pan, and unfold. Gently shift the dough around to settle it into the pan, then lightly press the dough further into place so that it is flush against the sides and bottom of the pan, including the outer edge. At the top edge of the pan, fold in any excess dough and gently form it into a slight lip level with the rim. Don't worry if it looks messy; it will puff up nicely when it bakes. Cover with plastic wrap and chill in the refrigerator or freezer until quite firm.

While the shell chills, preheat the oven to 375°F (190°C) with a rack in the center. Line a baking sheet with parchment paper and cut an additional piece of parchment or aluminum foil into a 16 x 16-inch square.

Line the shell with the parchment, gently smoothing and pleating the paper as needed to fit it into place up close against the bottom and sides of the crust. Fill to the rim with beans. Stick your fingers deep into the beans and gently push them around to ensure that there are no air pockets within the beans or between the crust and the paper, especially down around the bottom edge. Top up with more beans as needed to come level with the top edge of the crust.

Set the pan on the parchment-lined baking sheet, slide the sheet into the oven, and bake the quiche shell 30 minutes, rotating halfway through the baking time.

Set the baking sheet on a wire rack and let the shell cool for 10 minutes. Set out a mixing bowl alongside the rack. Bring together the points of the parchment (which won't be hot to the touch) to carefully lift out the beans and deposit them in the bowl.

Slide the baking sheet back into the oven and bake the shell another 10 minutes, or until golden. Cool the quiche shell on a wire rack before proceeding with the quiche recipe of your choice.

dough rounds for hand pies

If same-day pie is a must-have, hand pies are the way to go. Unlike a Magpie full-size pie, hand pies can be served up within minutes of baking. Because the volume of each pie is so much smaller it doesn't need the overnight rest to set up properly. Bonus about hand pies: They are the only Magpie pie that can be filled and then frozen (instructions follow). See page 82 for Strawberry Rhubarb Hand Pies, page 189 for Cookie Dough Hand Pies, and page 227 for a variety of suggestions for improvising your own savory hand pies.

◆ MAKES 8 ROUNDS OF DOUGH ◆

1 recipe Magpie Dough for Flaky Piecrust (page 17), chilled overnight

Line a baking sheet with parchment paper.

Lightly flour a smooth work surface and a rolling pin.

Take one chilled disk of dough out of the fridge. Give it a couple of firm squeezes, then unwrap it and set it on the floured work surface.

Set the pin crosswise on the dough and press down firmly, making a nice deep channel across the full width of the disk (fig. 1, page 21). Turn the disk 180 degrees and repeat, making a second indentation, forming a plus sign (fig. 2, page 21).

Use your rolling pin to press down each of the wedges, turning the dough 45 degrees each time. This will give you the beginnings of a thick circle (fig. 3, page 21).

Now, rolling from the center outward and rotating the dough a quarter turn to maintain a circular shape, roll the dough out to a 13-inch circle with an even thickness of ¼ inch (figs. 4–9, page 21; see Tips for Dough-Friendly Rolling, page 28).

Cut out four 4-inch rounds. Reserve the scraps for another use (see Scrap Dough, page 31). Set the rounds on the parchment-lined baking sheet, cover with plastic wrap, and transfer to the refrigerator.

Repeat the process with the second disk of dough. Fetch the baking sheet from the refrigerator, lay a sheet of parchment over the first set of dough rounds and lay the second set of rounds on top. Cover with plastic wrap and chill the rounds in the refrigerator 15 to 20 minutes before filling and baking, or layer the rounds with parchment paper, double-wrap in plastic, and freeze for up to 3 months. (Thaw the rounds overnight in the refrigerator, or for an hour or two at room temperature, before filling and baking.)

Follow your hand pie recipe's instructions for filling and baking.

CHAPTER

fruity pies

·······⟨⟩·······

ONE OF THE GREATEST JOYS OF HAVING MY VERY OWN PIE SHOP IS BAKING AND SERVING UP PIES FILLED WITH THE FRUITS THAT ARE IN SEASON *RIGHT NOW*.

Here in the Philadelphia area (hardiness zone 7a/7b), apples, pears, cranberries, and lemons and limes (thank you, Florida and Mexico) get us through the winter. Rhubarb, that stalky harbinger of spring, comes along sometime in April (and, stewed up with lots of sugar, passes for a fruit), and before too much longer it's joined by the first round of local strawberries, which properly kick off the annual return of sweet, juicy local fruit into our lives—and our pies.

Sour cherries, precious and increasingly rare gems, come and go in the blink of an eye, roundabout late May or early June. From then on, it is full-on fruit season—sweet cherries give way to blueberries; then come the peaches, raspberries (round one), and apricots; followed by the blackberries, plums, and raspberries (round two).

It all builds to a crescendo of bodacious bounty in August and winds down sometime in September, when heat and humidity loosen their grip, evenings get cooler, cicadas give way to crickets, and roadside farmstand offerings narrow down to early varieties of pears and apples, squash and pumpkins galore, and lots and lots of mums.

When I was growing up, my grandparents grew a lot of fruit out back in their mini orchard. We'd harvest each fruit just as it ripened on the tree and much pie-baking would ensue. We would pick berries in vast quantities at area farms so that there would always be enough

to freeze. That's really the best way to go: Hit the pick-your-own farms for cherries and berries. Freeze on baking sheets (pit the cherries first), then transfer to freezer bags. This is a much better way to enjoy the occasional midwinter blueberry or cherry pie—the flavor is much superior to anything you can buy frozen in the store.

A Magpie cardinal rule: Fruit pies *must* sit overnight (meaning a full 8 to 12 hours). Seriously. I kid you not. Follow this rule and you will never again go to the trouble of making a lovely fruit pie only to have it fall apart when you cut into it. Happy exceptions are mini pies and hand pies, so these are the ones to make on shorter notice: Apple Cherry Peanut Butter Mini Pies (page 53), Raspberry Mini Pies (page 99), Cranberry Curd Mini Meringue Pies (page 61), and Strawberry Rhubarb Hand Pies (page 82).

Adapting any of the simpler, non-custard fruit pie fillings for use in mini pies or hand pies is as simple as cutting the fruit up into a small dice, so that the filling will fit snugly in the little shells. Assemble and bake as directed on page 54 (mini pies) or page 82 (hand pies). Note that fruit-filled hand pies are the only pies I'd recommend freezing after filling. For best results, thaw 30 minutes at room temperature, glaze with egg wash and sprinkle with sugar, and add as much time as needed to the baking time to brown the shells and get the filling bubbling through the vent.

FOOLPROOF FRUIT FILLING

Fruit contains a lot of water, so just about every fruit pie needs some manner of thickener in the filling. Apples and pears contain pectin, a natural thickener, so a bit of cornstarch is all that's needed. But softer fruits like berries and peaches need something with a bit more jelling power. Through a *lot* of experimentation, I have found that instant tapioca is the wonder ingredient that, finely ground and used in combination with a bit of cornstarch, makes for the best berry and other soft-fruit fillings—beautifully glossy, perfectly set, and never cloudy or gelatinous.

Unlike cornstarch, tapioca does not break down when mixed with acidic ingredients or cooked for a long time. And unlike some of the specialty products used by professional bakers, instant tapioca is easy to come by (Kraft Minute Tapioca, which is what we use at the shop, is sold at just about every supermarket in North America. Note that instant tapioca is *not* the same as regular tapioca, which has larger beads, or tapioca pearls, which are even larger).

Before measuring the instant tapioca and adding it to the pie filling, you have to pulverize it in a coffee grinder or spice grinder; otherwise, the small starchy granules would become tiny gelatinous beads throughout your filling. For convenience, you can grind up several pies' worth—or even the whole box—and keep it in an airtight jar with your baking supplies.

Be sure to follow each pie recipe's instructions for mixing the ground instant tapioca with the other filling ingredients, then let the mixture sit for several minutes so the tapioca can start to absorb some of the liquid and begin to soften. This resting time also helps the sugar to start dissolving. For best results, have your fruit at room temperature rather than cold from the fridge.

The other crucial part of the thickening process happens in the oven; it is essential that the fruit filling cooks as described in each pie recipe, bubbling vigorously.

caramel apple pie

A combination of sweet and tart apples makes for a delicious pie. We grind a bit of pink peppercorn into the filling for nice citrus and spice notes, and we serve each slice with a scoop of buttermilk ice cream and a good drizzling of homemade caramel sauce. Heavenly.

◆ MAKES 1 (9-inch / 23-cm) PIE ◆

1 recipe Magpie Dough for Flaky Piecrust (page 17), chilled overnight

1½ pounds / 680 g Granny Smith apples, peeled, cored, and sliced ¼ inch thick

1½ pounds / 680 g Honeycrisp, Gala, Golden Delicious, or other firm, crisp, sweet-tart apples, peeled, cored, and sliced ¼ inch thick

1 tablespoon freshly squeezed lemon juice

½ cup / 96 g granulated sugar

2 tablespoons cornstarch

Pinch fine salt

2 teaspoons ground cinnamon

¼ teaspoon ground or freshly grated nutmeg

¼ teaspoon freshly ground pink peppercorn

1 large egg yolk

2 tablespoons sanding sugar or coarse raw sugar, for sprinkling

Buttermilk Ice Cream (page 121) or vanilla ice cream, for serving

Caramel Sauce (page 49), for serving

Follow the instructions on page 27 to roll and pan the bottom crust and the sheet of dough for the top crust. Transfer the pan and the baking sheet to the refrigerator to chill the dough while you make the filling.

Preheat the oven to 400°F (200°C) with a rack in the center. Line a rimmed baking sheet with parchment paper.

In a large bowl, toss the apple slices with the lemon juice. In a small bowl, whisk together the granulated sugar, cornstarch, salt, cinnamon, nutmeg, and pink pepper. Sprinkle the sugar mixture over the apples and toss well to coat the fruit and thoroughly moisten the cornstarch and sugar so that no dry white streaks remain.

(Continued)

Retrieve the prepared bottom crust from the refrigerator and set the pan on the parchment-lined baking sheet. Layer the apples into the pie shell with your hands, tightly stacking the slices into a level, flat-topped mound (see photo on page 47; a peaked mound will result in an empty air pocket after the pie is baked). Use your index finger to scrape some of the syrupy fruit juices off the sides of the mixing bowl and generously moisten the top edge of the shell.

Fetch the prepared top crust from the refrigerator and follow the instructions on page 27 to transfer the sheet of dough to the top of the pie and trim the edges. Gently pinch the edges of the dough together, folding under and tucking securely inside the lip of the pan.

In a small bowl, whisk the egg yolk with 1 tablespoon water. Lightly brush the top of the pie with the egg wash and sprinkle with the raw sugar. If you haven't already cut decorative vent holes, use a small, sharp knife or kitchen shears to cut 4 slits, each about 2 inches long, toward the center of the dough.

Transfer the baking sheet to the oven and bake the pie 20 minutes, then rotate the sheet and bake 22 to 25 minutes more, or until the crust is golden, the fruit is tender (the tip of a small, sharp knife can easily be inserted into the fruit through the vent holes), and the juices are bubbling up through the vent holes.

Transfer the baking sheet to a wire rack and let the pie cool and set uncovered, at room temperature, overnight (or up to 3 days), before slicing and serving.

Serve at room temperature, or rewarmed in a 425°F (220°C) oven, with ice cream and caramel.

spin

Caramel Pear Apple Pie:
Replace the sweet-tart apples with pears and add ½ cup (72 g) golden raisins.

caramel sauce

This caramel sauce keeps well in an airtight jar in the fridge. Use the extra to top ice cream.

◆ **MAKES 1½ CUPS** ◆

2 cups / 400 g granulated sugar

¾ cup / 170 g unsalted butter

1¼ cups / 295 g heavy cream, at room temperature

3 teaspoons vanilla extract

2 teaspoons kosher salt

Pour the sugar into a medium, high-sided saucepan, tilting the pan to distribute the sugar evenly across the bottom of the pan. Set the pan over medium-high heat. Use a rubber spatula to occasionally push the sugar from the outer edge of the pan toward the center. The sugar will clump up slightly, but just keep pushing it around a bit; it will eventually smooth out. When the sugar is dissolved and darkened to the color of a copper penny (about 5 to 7 minutes), add the butter and whisk until incorporated. Be careful: When you add the butter, the mixture will bubble up and might even seem like it's about to overflow the pan; just keep whisking and it will quickly settle back down.

Take the pan off the heat and carefully add the cream in two stages, whisking until smooth and incorporated. Add the vanilla and salt, whisking to combine.

Pour the caramel through a fine-mesh sieve into a bowl and cool completely to room temperature, about 2 hours, before using or transferring to an airtight container to store in the refrigerator. Return to room temperature before using.

apple cranberry walnut lattice pie

Using wide lattice strips brushed with egg wash but without any sugar sprinkled on top gives this pie a gorgeous, burnished mahogany look. The combination of apple, orange, cranberries, toasted walnuts, and cinnamon is very autumnal. Each morsel is like taking a bite of fall.

MAKES 1 (9-inch / 23-cm) PIE

1 recipe Magpie Dough for Flaky Piecrust (page 17), chilled overnight

2 pounds / 906 g sweet-tart apples (such as Honeycrisp or Gala), peeled, cored, and sliced ¼ inch thick

4 ounces / 113 g fresh cranberries

2 teaspoons freshly grated orange zest

1 tablespoon freshly squeezed orange juice

¾ cup / 144 g granulated sugar

2 tablespoons cornstarch

½ teaspoon ground cinnamon

⅛ teaspoon fine salt

½ cup / 50 g walnut pieces, toasted and finely chopped

1 large egg yolk

Maple Bourbon Ice Cream (page 124), for serving

Roll and pan the dough for the bottom crust as directed on page 29; follow the instructions on page 31 to roll and cut six 2-inch-wide lattice strips for the top of the pie. Transfer the pan and the baking sheet to the refrigerator and chill the dough while you make the filling.

Preheat the oven to 400°F (200°C) with a rack in the center. Line a rimmed baking sheet with parchment paper.

In a large bowl, toss the apples and cranberries with the orange zest and orange juice.

In a small bowl, whisk together the sugar, cornstarch, cinnamon, salt,

(Continued)

and walnuts. Sprinkle the sugar mixture over the fruit and toss to coat the fruit and moisten the sugar and cornstarch so that no dry white streaks remain.

Retrieve the prepared bottom crust from the refrigerator, set the pan on the parchment-lined baking sheet and evenly layer the apples into the pie shell with your hands, keeping the top of the filling flat and level (not peaked). Use your index finger to scrape some of the syrupy fruit juices off the sides of the mixing bowl and generously moisten the top edge of the shell.

Fetch the dough strips from the refrigerator and follow the instructions on page 31 to lattice the top of the pie and roll and crimp the edge. Whisk the egg yolk with 1 tablespoon water. Lightly brush the lattice with the egg wash.

Transfer the baking sheet to the oven and bake the pie 25 minutes at 400°F (200°C), then lower the oven temperature to 350°F (175°C), rotate the baking sheet and bake 25 to 30 minutes more, or until the lattice is golden and the fruit is tender (the tip of a small knife can easily be inserted into the fruit through the spaces in the lattice) and the juices are bubbling up through the lattice. Tent the top with foil if the crust starts to over-brown.

Transfer the baking sheet to a wire rack and let the pie cool and set uncovered, at room temperature, overnight (or up to 3 days) before slicing and serving. Serve at room temperature, or rewarmed in a 425°F (220°C) oven, with maple bourbon ice cream.

apple cherry peanut butter mini pies

Cookie-like peanut butter oatmeal crumb is my favorite topping for these delectable sweet-tart mini pies, but there are plenty of other great options: Oatmeal Crumb (page 57), Polenta Streusel (page 90), and Almond Crumb (page 85), to name just a few.

MAKES 12 (3-inch / 8-cm) MINI PIES

1 recipe Magpie Dough for Flaky Piecrust (page 17), chilled overnight

Peanut Butter Oatmeal Crumb (page 55), unbaked

1 pound / 453 g Granny Smith apples, peeled, cored, and cut into ¼-inch dice

¼ cup dried cherries, chopped

1 tablespoon freshly squeezed lemon juice

¼ cup / 50 g granulated sugar

1 tablespoon cornstarch

1½ teaspoons ground cinnamon

⅛ teaspoon ground or freshly grated nutmeg

Pinch fine salt

Lightly sweetened freshly whipped cream or vanilla ice cream, for serving

Roll and pan the dough as directed for mini pie shells (page 32). Transfer the muffin tin to the refrigerator and chill the shells while you make the crumb and the filling.

Prepare the crumb as directed on page 55. Transfer the bowl to the refrigerator and chill the crumb while you make the filling.

Preheat the oven to 375°F (190°C) with a rack in the center.

In a large bowl, toss the apples and cherries with the lemon juice.

In a small bowl, whisk together the sugar, cornstarch, spices, and salt.

(Continued)

53

Sprinkle the sugar mixture over the fruit and toss to coat the fruit and moisten the sugar and cornstarch so that no dry, white streaks remain.

Retrieve the prepared pie shells from the refrigerator. Distribute the filling evenly among the shells, then divide the chilled crumb among the pies, topping each with an even layer and covering all of the fruit.

Transfer the muffin pan to the oven and bake the pies 20 to 25 minutes, or until the crust is golden and the fruit juices bubble up through the crumb topping, rotating the pan halfway through the baking time.

Set the muffin pan on a wire rack and let the pies cool completely before using a butter knife to carefully lift each pie out of the muffin pan. Let the pies sit, uncovered, at room temperature at least 4 hours (or up to 3 days) before serving. Serve at room temperature with whipped cream or vanilla ice cream.

Apple Cherry Mini Pies: Replace the peanut butter oatmeal crumb topping with little baked cutouts. Roll out fresh or scrap dough (scrap is best, see page 31) to ¼-inch thickness and use a small cutter to make twelve shapes (plain or ruffle-edged circle, leaf, etc.). Set the shapes on a parchment-lined baking sheet, brush with egg wash, sprinkle with sanding sugar or cinnamon sugar, and bake at 350°F (175°C) for 10 to 12 minutes. Transfer the baking sheet to a wire rack and let the cutouts cool to room temperature before using a thin spatula to transfer them to the tops of the baked pies.

peanut butter oatmeal crumb

This crumb is like a layer of peanut butter cookie with an oaty texture. The prebaked version can be made ahead and deployed to turn Peanut Butter and Jam Pie (page 137) into Nutter Butter Pie (page 138; the crumb softens up as it sits, so when it's paired with peanut butter filling, it makes for a pie that really does taste like a Nutter Butter cookie). For another nice swap-in, see Chocolate Peanut Butter Mousse Pie (page 147). If you are using the crumb unbaked as a topping for Apple Cherry Peanut Butter Mini Pies (page 53) or another fruit pie and end up with more than you need, I highly recommend baking off the remainder and using it as a topping for ice cream.

 MAKES ABOUT 2 CUPS; ENOUGH TO TOP 1 (9-inch / 23-cm) **PIE OR 12** (3-inch / 8-cm) **MINI PIES**

1 cup / 80 g rolled oats, divided

½ cup / 62 g all-purpose flour

½ cup / 96 g packed light brown sugar

½ teaspoon ground cinnamon

½ teaspoon fine salt

2 tablespoons unsalted butter

6 tablespoons / 96 g peanut butter

Use a food processor to grind ¾ cup of the oats, pulsing the machine until the oats resemble coarse cornmeal. Add the flour, sugar, cinnamon, and salt, and pulse 5 times to combine. Transfer the mixture to a medium bowl and whisk in the remaining ¼ cup whole oats.

In a small saucepan, combine the butter and the peanut butter and melt together over medium-low heat until smooth, stirring occasionally.

Pour the peanut butter mixture into the oat mixture and use a fork or your fingers to blend the ingredients until small clumps form. Chill the crumb for 15 minutes.

To top a fruit pie: Layer on the chilled crumb just before baking.

To top a cream pie: While the crumb is chilling, preheat the oven to 350°F (175°C) with a rack in the center and line a baking sheet with parchment paper. Evenly scatter the chilled crumb on the baking sheet. Bake 7 to 8 minutes, or until lightly golden. Transfer the baking sheet to a wire rack and leave the crumb on the baking sheet to cool completely. Spread the cooled crumb evenly on top of the pie, or store in an airtight container for up to 5 days.

pear ginger oatmeal crumb pie

Pears first come into season at the end of summer, just before all but the earliest apple varieties. This pie is one of the Magpie treats that makes us a little less sad to bid farewell to all the juicy fruits of summer, and we serve it up from late summer throughout fall and into the holiday season. The zing of candied ginger perks up the soft sweetness of the pears, and oatmeal crumb topping adds a little crunch and warm nutmeg fragrance.

MAKES 1 (9-inch / 23-cm) PIE

½ recipe Magpie Dough for Flaky Piecrust (page 17), chilled overnight

Oatmeal Crumb (page 57)

2½ pounds / 1132 g firm, ripe, unpeeled Bartlett pears, cored and sliced ⅛ inch thick

1 tablespoon freshly squeezed lemon juice

2 teaspoons vanilla extract

⅓ cup / 63 g granulated sugar

2 tablespoons cornstarch

2 tablespoons minced candied ginger

⅛ teaspoon fine salt

Ginger Ice Cream (page 123), for serving

Roll and pan the dough as directed for a Single-Crust Pie Shell (page 20–23). Transfer the pan to the refrigerator to chill the dough while you make the crumb and the filling.

Prepare the oatmeal crumb as directed on page 57. Transfer the bowl to the refrigerator to chill the topping while you make the filling.

Preheat the oven to 375°F (190°C) with a rack in the center. Line a rimmed baking sheet with parchment paper.

In a large bowl, toss the pears with the lemon juice and vanilla.

In a small bowl, whisk together the sugar, cornstarch, candied ginger, and salt. Sprinkle the sugar mixture over the pears and toss to coat the fruit and moisten the sugar and cornstarch so that no dry white streaks remain.

Retrieve the prepared pie shell from the refrigerator and set the pan on the parchment-lined baking sheet. Scoop the filling into the shell and top with the oatmeal crumb, spreading evenly and completely covering the fruit.

Transfer the baking sheet to the oven and bake the pie 25 minutes, then rotate the baking sheet, lower the oven temperature to 350°F (175°C), and bake 25 to 30 minutes more, or until the topping is golden and the juices bubble up through the crumb. Tent the top with foil if it starts to over-brown.

Set the baking sheet on a wire rack and let the pie cool and set, uncovered, at room temperature, overnight (or up to 3 days) before slicing and serving with ginger ice cream.

oatmeal crumb

This is a great crumb base, easily adaptable and open to improvisation, depending on the ingredients you have in your cupboard and the kind of pie you're topping. Feel free to switch out white sugar for brown sugar, replace the ¼ cup of unground oats with chopped nuts, or play around with different spices. The crumb can be made in advance and stored in an airtight container in the fridge for a week or frozen for a month.

MAKES ABOUT 2 CUPS; ENOUGH TO TOP 1 (9-inch / 23-cm) **PIE OR 12** (3-inch / 8-cm) **MINI PIES**

1 cup / 80 g rolled oats, divided

½ cup / 62 g all-purpose flour

½ cup / 96 g granulated sugar

1 teaspoon ground ginger

¼ teaspoon ground or freshly grated nutmeg

¼ teaspoon kosher salt

5 tablespoons / 71 g unsalted butter, melted and cooled

Use a food processor to grind ¾ cup of the oats, pulsing the machine until the oats resemble coarse cornmeal. Add the flour, sugar, ginger, nutmeg, and salt and pulse 5 times to combine. Transfer the mixture to a bowl and whisk in the remaining ¼ cup whole oats.

Add the melted butter and blend with a fork or your fingers until the butter is incorporated and the mixture gathers into small clumps. Set the bowl in the refrigerator and chill the crumb for 15 minutes before topping your pie.

pear chocolate pie

Pears and chocolate are an ultra-complementary combination of flavors, aromas, and textures—delicate yet voluptuous. Together they make a downright swoony pie. You'll need about eight medium-sized pears and a bar of very good bittersweet chocolate.

MAKES 1 (9-inch / 23-cm) PIE

1 recipe Magpie Dough for Flaky Piecrust (page 17), chilled overnight

2½ pounds /1132 g firm, ripe, unpeeled Bartlett pears, cored and sliced ⅛ inch thick

1 tablespoon freshly squeezed lemon juice

1 tablespoon vanilla extract

⅓ cup / 63 g granulated sugar

2 tablespoons cornstarch

⅛ teaspoon fine salt

4 ounces bittersweet chocolate, finely chopped

1 large egg yolk

2 tablespoons sanding sugar or coarse raw sugar, for sprinkling

Follow the instructions on page 27 to roll and pan the bottom crust and the sheet of dough for the top crust. Transfer the pan and the baking sheet to the refrigerator to chill the dough while you make the filling.

Preheat the oven to 400°F (200°C) with a rack in the center. Line a rimmed baking sheet with parchment paper.

In a large bowl, toss the pears with the lemon juice and vanilla.

In a small bowl, whisk together the granulated sugar, cornstarch, and salt. Sprinkle the sugar mixture over the pears and toss to coat the fruit and moisten the sugar and cornstarch so that no dry, white streaks remain.

Retrieve the prepared bottom crust from the refrigerator and set the pan on the parchment-lined baking sheet. Spread the chopped chocolate evenly across the bottom of the pie shell and top with the pear filling. Use your index finger to scrape some of the syrupy fruit juices off the sides of the mixing bowl and generously moisten the top edge of the shell.

Follow the instructions on pages 27–28 to cut decorative vent holes or slits in the top crust, transfer it onto the pie, and trim and crimp the edges. Whisk the egg yolk with 1 tablespoon water. Lightly brush the crust with the egg wash and sprinkle with sanding sugar.

Transfer the baking sheet to the oven and bake the pie for 25 minutes at 400°F (200°C), then rotate the baking sheet, lower the oven temperature to 350°F (175°C), and bake 25 to 30 minutes more, or until the top is golden and the juices bubble up through the vent holes. Tent with foil if the crust starts to over-brown. Let the pie cool and set, uncovered, at room temperature, overnight (or up to 3 days) before slicing and serving.

cranberry curd mini meringue pies

Cranberries: so good and so underused! This lovely seasonal fruit is readily available in supermarkets throughout North America from mid-September through November, and way too delicious to be relished only in sauces and condiments. I love to throw cranberries into pies along with other fruit, but they also hold their own beautifully. Here the berries make a gorgeous curd, with big flavor power from their innate tartness and great consistency from their natural pectin. Condensed milk brings sweet creaminess and lightens the color from dark garnet to deep blush pink. These pies are very refreshing at the end of a big meal—the perfect conclusion to a holiday feast. Feel free to top them with whipped cream instead of meringue.

MAKES 12 (3-inch / 8-cm) PIES

1 recipe Magpie Dough for Flaky Piecrust (page 17), chilled overnight

2 (12-ounce) bags fresh cranberries

4 large egg yolks

1 (14-ounce / 297 g) can sweetened condensed milk

⅓ cup / 83 ml freshly squeezed orange juice

½ teaspoon freshly grated orange zest

1 tablespoon brandy

Pinch fine salt

1 recipe Vanilla Meringue (page 63)

Follow the directions on page 32 to roll and pan the piecrusts for mini pies, then prebake as directed. Set the muffin tin on a wire rack and let the shells cool to room temperature while you make the filling.

Preheat the oven to 350°F (175°C) with a rack in the center. Line a rimmed baking sheet with parchment paper.

Combine the cranberries and ¾ cup water in a small saucepan and bring to a boil over medium-high heat. Lower the heat to medium and cook 10 minutes, or until the berries have burst, stirring occasionally.

(Continued)

Let the fruit cool slightly, then transfer it to a food processor and purée until smooth. Set a fine-mesh sieve over a medium bowl and press the purée through the sieve (discard solids left in sieve).

Whisk the egg yolks and sweetened condensed milk together in a large bowl. Add the orange juice and zest, cranberry purée, brandy, and salt; whisk until smooth and uniform. Set the pan of prebaked shells on the parchment-lined baking sheet. Divide the filling evenly among the shells and bake 12 to 15 minutes, or until set.

Set the baking sheet on a wire rack and let the pies cool completely to room temperature. In the meantime, make the meringue. Generously top each cooled pie with meringue (you can spoon it on and swirl with a rubber spatula, or pipe it on with a pastry bag).

To toast the meringue, position the oven shelf one level below the topmost rung. Preheat the broiler to low. Slide the baking sheet under the broiler for 30 seconds to 1 minute and toast just until the meringue is browned on top. Let cool to room temperature, then use a butter knife to carefully lift each pie out of the muffin pan. Chill, uncovered, at least 4 hours and up to 2 days before serving.

vanilla meringue

We use an Italian-style meringue (boiling sugar syrup poured slowly into softly whipped egg whites and beaten until stiff), which holds up extremely well, so the topped pies keep nicely for a few days. Note, however, that damp days are not ideal for making meringue, no matter what method you use.

◄ MAKES ENOUGH TO TOP 1 (9-inch / 23-cm) PIE OR 12 (3-inch / 8-cm) MINI PIES ►

¾ cup / 144 g granulated sugar

3 egg whites, at room temperature

¼ teaspoon cream of tartar

Pinch fine salt

½ vanilla bean

½ teaspoon vanilla extract

Combine the sugar with ¼ cup water in a small saucepan and bring to a boil over medium heat. Continue boiling the mixture undisturbed until it registers 240°F (115°C) on a candy thermometer, 5 to 10 minutes. Keep warm over very low heat.

Combine the egg whites, cream of tartar, and salt in the bowl of a stand mixer fitted with a whisk attachment. Beat the mixture at medium-low speed until it is foamy, about 2 minutes, then turn the speed up to medium-high and whip until it is shiny and forms soft peaks, 5 to 7 minutes (see Whipping Egg Whites, page 132).

Lower the mixer speed to medium and slowly add the hot syrup, pouring in a thin stream and taking care not to let the stream of syrup hit the side of the bowl on its way in (this will cause it to harden instantly).

Use a small, sharp knife to split the vanilla bean lengthwise and scrape the sticky seeds into the meringue mixture. Add vanilla extract and turn the mixer speed back up to medium-high and whip the meringue until it is very thick, very glossy, and the bottom of the bowl is cool to the touch, 8 to 10 minutes.

hummingbird pie

The inspiration for this pie is hummingbird cake, a Southern classic traditionally made with canned pineapple. We use fresh pineapple, which, along with bananas, dried apricots, and a crumb topping made with coconut, pecans, and cinnamon, heightens the lush feel. In the dead of winter, a slice of this pie is like a quick trip to the sweet South.

◄ MAKES 1 (9-inch / 23-cm) PIE ►

½ recipe Magpie Dough for Flaky Piecrust (page 17), chilled overnight

Coconut Pecan Crumb (page 66)

½ cup / 96 g packed light brown sugar

1 tablespoon cornstarch

¼ teaspoon ground nutmeg

1 teaspoon ground cinnamon

⅛ teaspoon fine salt

1 small pineapple, cored, peeled, and cut into ½-inch pieces (3 cups)

2 bananas, peeled and cut into ¼-inch-thick slices

¼ cup / 42 g diced dried apricots

2 tablespoons freshly squeezed lemon juice

2 tablespoons Jamaican rum

Vanilla ice cream, for serving

Roll, pan, and flute the dough for a single-crust pie as directed on pages 20–23. Set the pan in the refrigerator and chill the shell. Prepare the crumb as instructed on page 66 and chill it in the refrigerator.

Preheat the oven to 375°F (190°C) with a rack in the center. Line a rimmed baking sheet with parchment paper.

Whisk the brown sugar, cornstarch, nutmeg, cinnamon, and salt together in a small bowl.

In a large bowl, combine the pineapple, bananas, dried apricots, lemon juice, and rum, tossing lightly to mix. Sprinkle in the sugar mixture and toss well, coating the fruit and thoroughly moistening the cornstarch and sugar.

Retrieve the prepared pie shell from the refrigerator and set the pan on the parchment-lined baking sheet. Scoop the filling into the pie shell and top with the crumb. Transfer the baking sheet to the oven and bake the pie 25 minutes, then rotate the baking sheet, lower the oven temperature to 350°F (175°C), and bake another 25 to 30 minutes, or until the juices are bubbling. Tent the top with foil if the crumb starts to over-brown.

Set the baking sheet on a wire rack and let the pie cool and set, uncovered, at room temperature overnight (or up to 3 days), before slicing and serving with vanilla ice cream.

coconut pecan crumb

We created this crumb especially for our Hummingbird Pie, but it would also make a fantastic topping for Caramel Apple Pie (instead of the top crust; page 46) or Pear Ginger (rather than the oatmeal crumb; page 56).

MAKES ABOUT 2 CUPS; ENOUGH TO TOP 1 (9-inch / 23-cm) **PIE OR 12** (2-inch / 8-cm) **MINI PIES**

¼ cup / 20 g rolled oats

½ cup / 62 g all-purpose flour

5 tablespoons / 56 g packed light brown sugar

1 teaspoon ground cinnamon

½ teaspoon ground ginger

⅛ teaspoon ground or freshly grated nutmeg

⅛ teaspoon fine salt

6 tablespoons / 85 g unsalted butter, melted and cooled

¼ cup / 20 g pecan pieces

½ cup / 57 g sweetened coconut flakes

Use a food processor to grind the oats, pulsing the machine until the oats resemble coarse cornmeal.

Whisk the ground oats, flour, sugar, cinnamon, ginger, nutmeg, and salt together in a medium bowl. Add the melted butter and mix with your fingers or a fork until small clumps form. Add the pecans and coconut and mix lightly. Chill the crumb for 15 minutes before topping the pie.

lemon gingersnap pie

Creamy lemon-ginger custard in a snappy spiced crust is the perfect ending to a rich meal. Top each slice with a dollop of freshly whipped cream to bring all of the piquant flavors into sweet harmony.

◆ **MAKES 1 (9-inch / 23-cm) PIE** ◆

1 recipe Gingersnap Crust (page 69)

3 large egg yolks

1 (14-ounce / 297g) can sweetened condensed milk

½ cup / 113 g freshly squeezed lemon juice

1 teaspoon peeled and grated fresh ginger

½ teaspoon ground ginger

1 teaspoon vanilla extract

Pinch of fine salt

Lightly sweetened freshly whipped cream, for serving

Prepare the gingersnap crust as directed on page 69. Set the pan in the refrigerator and chill the crust while you make the filling.

Preheat the oven to 325°F (160°C) with a rack in the center. Line a rimmed baking sheet with parchment paper. Use an electric mixer fitted with a whisk attachment to beat the yolks on medium speed until light and fluffy, about 3 minutes. Add the condensed milk and beat 3 minutes more. Turn the mixer speed down to low and, with the machine running, slowly add the lemon juice, pouring in a thin stream. When the mixture starts to thicken, in 2 to 3 minutes, add the fresh and ground ginger, vanilla, and salt and mix gently to incorporate.

Retrieve the prepared gingersnap crust from the refrigerator and set the pan on the prepared baking sheet. Pour the filling into the crust, smoothing the top. Carefully transfer the baking sheet to the oven and bake the pie 11 minutes, or until barely set (firm at the outer edges but still a bit wobbly in the very center).

Set the baking sheet on a wire rack and let the pie cool completely to room temperature, then cover with plastic wrap (don't let it touch the top of the filling) and chill overnight (at least 12 hours and up to 3 days) before slicing and serving. Serve cold with whipped cream.

gingersnap crust

Our gingersnap crust is a simple combination of graham cracker crumbs, dark brown sugar, cinnamon, ginger, cloves, freshly ground black pepper, and butter. Its deep brown color, delicate texture, and aromatic flavor make it a beautiful vessel for pale creamy fillings.

MAKES 1 (9-inch / 23-cm) CRUST

1 cup plus 2 tablespoons / 140 g packaged graham cracker crumbs

¼ cup / 55 g packed dark brown sugar

2 teaspoons ground cinnamon

2 teaspoons ground ginger

¼ teaspoon ground cloves

⅛ teaspoon finely ground black pepper

5 tablespoons / 70 g unsalted butter, melted

Whisk together the graham cracker crumbs, brown sugar, cinnamon, ginger, cloves, and black pepper in a medium bowl. Add the melted butter and 2 teaspoons water and blend with a fork or your fingers until the mixture holds together when squeezed. Press the crumb crust in an even layer across the bottom and up the sides of a 9-inch (23-cm) pie pan.

Chill the crust for 15 minutes before filling, or freeze until solid, then cover tightly in plastic wrap and keep in the freezer for up to 1 month (thaw overnight in the refrigerator or at room temperature for 1 hour before filling and baking).

lemon curd pie

Making the lemon curd filling is not difficult, but close attention is essential to cooking the mixture to the proper temperature; it can overheat and curdle surprisingly quickly. Here's how to make sure that doesn't happen: Once you have the saucepan on the stove, don't stop whisking for a moment. Have your instant-read thermometer close at hand so that you can dip it into the pan to check the temperature frequently as the mixture begins to thicken. This will enable you to catch the moment it hits that magic 160°F (70°C) mark and pull the pan off the heat right away. Then whisk in the butter and vanilla and delight in the silky, sumptuous, sunshine-yellow glory that is classic lemon curd.

◆ **MAKES 1 (9-inch / 23-cm) PIE** ◆

½ recipe Magpie Dough for Flaky Piecrust (page 17), chilled overnight

1¼ cups / 250 g granulated sugar

1 tablespoon cornstarch

⅛ teaspoon fine salt

6 large eggs

⅔ cup / 158 ml freshly squeezed lemon juice

½ cup /113 g unsalted butter, cut into small pieces, at room temperature

½ teaspoon vanilla extract

1 tablespoon freshly grated lemon zest

Lightly sweetened freshly whipped cream, for serving

Roll, pan, and flute the crust as directed on pages 20–23, then follow the instructions to fully prebake the shell. Set the pan on a wire rack and cool completely to room temperature while you make the filling.

Preheat the oven to 350°F (175°C) with a rack in the center. Line a baking sheet with parchment paper.

Whisk the sugar, cornstarch, and salt together in a medium saucepan. Whisk in the eggs until incorporated. Add the lemon juice and whisk until uniformly blended.

Set the saucepan over medium heat and cook the mixture, whisking constantly to prevent it from curdling, until it is pale and quite thick (it should look a lot like a hollandaise sauce) and registers 160°F (70°C) on an instant-read thermometer; this will take about 10 minutes.

Remove the pan from the heat, add the butter, and whisk the mixture until smooth. Whisk in the vanilla extract and lemon zest.

(Continued)

Set the prepared pie shell on the parchment-lined baking sheet. Pour the lemon curd into the shell, smoothing the top. Transfer the baking sheet to the oven and bake the pie 12 minutes, or just until the edges of the filling have puffed and the center is barely set.

Set the baking sheet on a wire rack and let the pie cool completely to room temperature, then cover with plastic wrap (don't allow the wrap to touch the surface of the filling) and chill overnight (at least 12 hours or up to 3 days) before slicing and serving. Serve cold with whipped cream.

Lemon Meringue Pie: Preheat the oven to 375°F (190°C). Top the cooled Lemon Curd Pie with Vanilla Meringue (page 63), spreading with a rubber spatula and creating decorative peaks and swirls by twisting and lifting the spatula (or use a pastry bag to pipe the meringue). Important: Take care to completely cover the filling and spread the meringue so that it touches the edges of the crust all the way around (this will ensure that it doesn't pull away from the sides as it sets, forming an island of meringue). Bake 8 to 10 minutes, or just until the meringue is golden (keep a very close eye on it!). Cool completely on a wire rack. Chill overnight (at least 12 hours and up to 3 days) before slicing and serving.

meyer lemon vanilla shaker pie

Meyer lemons have a thinner peel and a softer citrus flavor than regular lemons, and they are available from December through May in many supermarkets. Slicing the lemons paper-thin and macerating for 3 days softens and sweetens the rind. Even so, we always serve this gorgeous pie with vanilla ice cream to cut the tartness, and, fair warning, it is intense—best appreciated by true lovers of the lemon. At the shop, this is one of the double-crust pies that we top with sparkling sugar, which has large crystals that add extra twinkle; but regular sanding or coarse sugar (easier to find and less expensive) is plenty pretty as well.

◆ MAKES 1 (9-inch / 23-cm) PIE ◆

3 medium-size Meyer lemons, cut into paper-thin rounds, seeds removed

2 cups / 384 g granulated sugar

½ vanilla bean

1 recipe Magpie Dough for Flaky Piecrust (page 17), chilled overnight

½ teaspoon fine salt

2 large eggs

3 large egg yolks, divided

3 tablespoons / 24 g all-purpose flour

2 tablespoons sanding, coarse, or sparkling sugar, for sprinkling

Vanilla ice cream, for serving

In a medium bowl, toss the lemon slices with the granulated sugar. Use a small sharp knife to split the vanilla bean lengthwise and scrape the sticky seeds into the bowl. Add the vanilla bean pod, mix well, cover with plastic wrap, and let stand at room temperature for 3 days, stirring once or twice daily.

Follow the instructions on page 27 to roll and pan the dough for the top and bottom crust. Transfer the pan and the baking sheet to the refrigerator to chill while you finish making the filling.

Preheat the oven to 425°F (220°C) with a rack in the center.

Fish the vanilla bean pod out of the cured lemon mixture (which will now be very liquidy) and pour the mixture into the bowl of a food processor. Pulse the machine a few times, or until the lemon rinds look like small flakes. Pour the mixture back into the mixing bowl.

In a small bowl, whisk together the salt, the eggs, and 2 of the yolks. Sprinkle in the flour 1 tablespoon at a time, whisking continuously to prevent lumps from forming. Whisk the egg mixture into the lemon mixture until combined.

(Continued)

Retrieve the prepared bottom crust from the refrigerator and set the pan on a parchment-lined baking sheet. Pour the filling into the pie shell. Use your index finger to scrape some of the syrupy fruit juices off the sides of the mixing bowl and generously moisten the top edge of the shell.

Fetch the prepared top crust from the refrigerator. Follow the instructions on pages 27–28 to cut decorative vent holes or slits in the dough, transfer it onto the pie, and trim and crimp the edges. Carefully slide the baking tray back into the refrigerator and chill the pie for 15 minutes.

Whisk the remaining egg yolk with 1 tablespoon water. Lightly brush the top of the pie with the egg wash and sprinkle with sugar.

Carefully transfer the baking sheet to the oven and bake the pie 20 minutes, then rotate the baking sheet, lower the oven temperature to 350°F (175°C), and bake 20 to 25 minutes more, or until the crust is golden and has been puffed up by the filling (you'll know it when you see it).

Set the baking sheet on a wire rack and let the pie cool and set, uncovered, at room temperature, overnight (or up to 3 days) before slicing and serving with vanilla ice cream.

Note: Once you have cut into the pie, cover any leftovers with plastic wrap and keep in the refrigerator (to keep the filling solid) for up to 3 days.

lime custard pie with basil cream and pistachio praline

You'll be amazed how tangy lime and sweet basil complement each other. Note that the cream and the praline need to be made ahead.

◆ **MAKES 1 (9-inch / 23-cm) PIE** ◆

Basil Cream (page 76), for serving

Pistachio Praline (page 78), for serving

½ recipe Magpie Dough for Flaky Piecrust (page 17), chilled overnight

4 large egg yolks

1⅔ cups / 394 ml sweetened condensed milk

⅔ cup / 158 ml freshly squeezed lime juice

2½ teaspoons freshly grated lime zest

1 teaspoon ground ginger

Pinch fine salt

Prepare the basil cream and pistachio praline as directed on pages 76 and 78.

Roll, pan, and flute the dough as directed on pages 20–23. Follow the instructions on page 24 to fully prebake the shell. Set the pan on a wire rack and let the piecrust cool completely to room temperature while you make the filling.

Preheat the oven to 350°F (175°C) with a rack in the center. Line a rimmed baking sheet with parchment paper.

Put the yolks in a large bowl and use a handheld electric mixer to beat at medium-high speed until light and fluffy, about 3 minutes. Lower the mixer speed to medium, pour in the condensed milk, and beat for 4 minutes. Slowly add the lime juice, pouring in a thin stream and beating constantly until the mixture starts to thicken, about 1 minute. Add lime zest, ginger, and salt and mix on medium speed until smooth.

Set the prebaked piecrust on the parchment-lined baking sheet and pour the filling into the shell, smoothing the top. Carefully transfer the baking sheet to the oven and bake the pie 10 to 12 minutes, or until firm at the edges but still slightly jiggly at the center.

(Continued)

Transfer the baking sheet to a wire rack and let the pie cool completely to room temperature, then cover with plastic wrap and chill overnight (at least 12 hours and up to 3 days) before slicing and serving. Serve cold, each slice topped with a dollop of basil cream and plenty of pistachio praline.

basil cream

Heated just enough to sweeten with sugar, then infused with basil, chilled, and finally whipped to velvety peaks, this cream is a perfect accompaniment to the tart lime pie with pistachio praline. It is also delicious with fresh-picked strawberries, not to mention grilled peaches and plums.

MAKES 2 CUPS

1 cup / 237 ml heavy cream

2 tablespoons granulated sugar

¼ cup / 10 g fresh basil leaves

Combine the cream and sugar in a medium saucepan. Set the pan over medium-high heat and stir constantly until the mixture is steaming but not boiling.

Take the pan off the heat, tear the basil leaves into strips, and gently stir the strips into the hot cream. Cover the pan and let the mixture steep for 30 minutes.

Pour the infused cream through a fine-mesh strainer into a medium bowl and set the bowl in the refrigerator for several hours, or until very well chilled.

When the cream is thoroughly chilled, use a handheld mixer at high speed to whip the cream to medium peaks. Use the basil cream immediately or keep in an airtight container in the refrigerator for up to 3 days.

pistachio praline

This is a very basic brittle: you heat sugar to the candy stage and stir the nuts in; the mixture hardens in a matter of minutes and you chop it up into little nuggets. The bits of green pistachio suspended in amber sugar are a beautiful visual atop the lime custard pie.

◁ MAKES ABOUT 1 CUP ▷

5 tablespoons / 63 g
granulated sugar

2 teaspoons corn syrup

1 cup / 100 g roasted, salted
shelled pistachios

Line a cutting board with a silicone baking mat, or lightly grease a baking sheet.

Combine the sugar and corn syrup with 3 teaspoons water in a small saucepan. Stir together, then set the pan over medium-high heat and bring to a boil, undisturbed. Continue cooking without stirring until the mixture takes on a light golden color, 3 to 5 minutes.

Take the pan off the heat and quickly stir in the pistachios, mixing until the nuts are well coated with the syrup. Pour the mixture out onto the silicone mat and let cool completely. Transfer the praline to a cutting board and chop it into small pieces. Keep the praline in an airtight container at room temperature up to 1 week.

strawberry crumb pie

Strawberry pie is typically icebox-style, with a filling of glazed, uncooked strawberries. But a baked strawberry pie has the full-flavored sweetness of homemade strawberry jam. It took some time to get this recipe just right. The eventual breakthroughs were small exceptions to our usual approach to seasoning fruit to heighten flavor: This is the only Magpie fruit pie that has no salt in the filling. It does have lemon juice, our usual flavor booster for fruit pies, but it also includes orange zest, not for citrus taste, but to intensify the flavor of the strawberries.

MAKES 1 (9-inch / 23-cm) PIE

½ recipe Magpie Dough for Flaky Piecrust (page 17), chilled overnight

Brown Sugar Crumb (page 81)

2 pounds / 906 g strawberries, hulled and quartered

2 teaspoons freshly squeezed lemon juice

¼ teaspoon freshly grated orange zest

½ teaspoon vanilla extract

¾ cup / 144 g granulated sugar

¼ cup / 48 g finely ground instant tapioca (see page 45)

2 tablespoons cornstarch

Buttermilk Ice Cream (page 121), for serving

Follow the instructions on pages 20–23 to roll, pan, and flute the dough. Transfer the pan to the refrigerator to chill the crust while you make the crumb and filling.

Prepare the crumb as directed on page 81. Set the bowl in the refrigerator and chill the crumb while you make the filling.

Preheat the oven to 375°F (190°C). Line a rimmed baking sheet with parchment paper.

In a large bowl, toss the strawberries with the lemon juice, orange zest, and vanilla extract. Toss to combine.

Whisk the sugar, ground tapioca, and cornstarch together in a small bowl. Sprinkle the sugar mixture over the strawberries and toss to combine. The mixture may seem dry at first; let it sit 5 to 10 minutes, and the lemon and sugar will draw the juices out of the fruit. Then give the mixture another good tossing to thoroughly moisten all of the sugar and tapioca granules.

(Continued)

Retrieve the prepared crust and crumb from the refrigerator and set the pan on the parchment-lined baking sheet. Pour the filling into the pie shell. Top the pie with the crumb, spreading in an even layer and covering all of the fruit.

Transfer the baking sheet to the oven and bake 25 minutes, then reduce the oven temperature to 350°F (175°C) and bake 25 to 30 minutes more, or until the juices bubble up through the crumb. Tent the top with foil if the crumb or crust starts to over-brown.

Transfer the baking sheet to a wire rack and let the pie cool and set, uncovered, at room temperature, overnight (or up to 3 days) before slicing and serving with buttermilk ice cream.

brown sugar crumb

Having experimented with all sorts of crumbs and crusts, I can tell you that, as simple as it is, this is the absolute best topping for our jammy strawberry pie. You could not go wrong using this topping on virtually any kind of fruit pie in any season.

MAKES ABOUT 2 CUPS; ENOUGH TO TOP 1 (9-inch / 23-cm) PIE OR 12 (2-inch / 8-cm) MINI PIES

½ cup / 40 g rolled oats

½ cup / 62 g all-purpose flour

½ cup / 96 g packed light brown sugar

½ teaspoon ground cinnamon

¼ teaspoon fine salt

6 tablespoons / 85 g unsalted butter, melted and cooled

Put the oats in the bowl of a food processor and pulse the machine to grind the oats to the texture of coarse cornmeal. Add the flour, sugar, cinnamon, and salt and pulse the machine 5 times to combine.

Transfer the mixture to a medium bowl. Add the melted butter and blend with a fork or your fingers until the butter is incorporated and the mixture gathers into small clumps. Transfer the bowl to the refrigerator and chill the crumb for 5 to 10 minutes before topping a pie.

< MAGPIE >

strawberry rhubarb hand pies

Strawberry rhubarb pie—is there any dessert more deliciously representative of the first blush of early spring? Wrapping the sweet-tart combo in a little pastry pocket puts a fun, fresh spin on a traditional staple, and the prep is truly quick and easy, especially if you keep a full batch of flaky piecrust dough in your freezer at all times (always a good idea; see pages 189 and 227 for a bunch more tasty reasons).

◇ **MAKES 8 (4-inch / 10-cm) HAND PIES** ◇

1 recipe Magpie Dough for Flaky Piecrust (page 17), chilled overnight

4 ounces strawberries, hulled and quartered

4 ounces rhubarb, trimmed and cut into ½-inch pieces

1 teaspoon freshly squeezed lemon juice

4 teaspoons vanilla extract

½ cup / 96 g granulated sugar

2 tablespoons finely ground instant tapioca (see page 45)

½ teaspoon ground ginger

⅛ teaspoon fine salt

1 large egg yolk

Sanding sugar or coarse raw sugar, for sprinkling

Vanilla ice cream, for serving

Follow the instructions on pages 40–41 to roll and cut the dough for hand pies, transfer the dough circles to a parchment-lined baking sheet, and set in the refrigerator to chill while you make the filling.

In a large bowl, toss the strawberries and rhubarb with the lemon juice and vanilla extract.

In a small bowl, whisk together the granulated sugar, ground tapioca, ginger, and salt. Sprinkle the sugar mixture over the fruit, and toss to combine. The mixture may seem dry at first; let it sit 10 minutes, and the lemon juice and sugar will draw the juices out of the fruit. Then give the mixture another good tossing to thoroughly moisten all of the sugar and tapioca granules.

Whisk the egg yolk with 1 tablespoon water. Retrieve the baking sheet from the refrigerator. Brush the edges of the dough circles with egg wash. Divide the filling among the eight circles, centering about 2 tablespoons of filling on each circle. Fold the dough over the filling and press the edges together. Using a fork, gently press the edges to seal.

Transfer the baking sheet to the refrigerator and chill the pies for 15 minutes. Lightly brush the tops of the pies with egg wash and sprinkle with sanding sugar. Use a small knife or kitchen shears to cut a ½-inch slit in the top of each pie. (Alternatively, freeze the pies on the baking sheet until solid, then transfer to freezer bags; thaw 30 minutes before baking.)

Preheat the oven to 400°F (200°C) with a rack in the center.

Transfer the chilled pies to the oven and bake 22 to 25 minutes, or until the crusts are golden brown and the juices start to bubble out through the vent holes. Let cool 15 minutes before serving with vanilla ice cream.

sour cherry almond crumb pie

When I was a kid, my grandmother would call whenever fruit was ready, and over we would troop to my grandparents' backyard mini orchard to pick. I loved to thread the stem of a bright red sour cherry between my fingers and pretend it was a giant ruby ring. I loved it even more when my mother got to baking her world-class sour cherry pie. To this day it is my favorite. Sour cherries have a very brief season in late spring or early summer, and it's getting harder to come by fresh ones in most places. If you do find them fresh, buy loads of them to pit and freeze. If not, you should be able to find frozen sour cherries if you call around to a few grocery stores. Either way, if you're using frozen cherries, partially thaw them so that there's some juice for the tapioca-sugar mixture to blend with.

◄ **MAKES 1 (9-inch / 23-cm) PIE** ►

½ recipe Magpie Dough for Flaky Piecrust (page 17), chilled overnight

Almond Crumb (page 85)

2 pounds / 906 g fresh sour cherries, pitted, or 1¾ pounds frozen pitted cherries, partially thawed

1 teaspoon freshly squeezed lemon juice

1 teaspoon almond extract

½ cup / 96 g granulated sugar

1 teaspoon cornstarch

3 tablespoons finely ground instant tapioca (see page 45)

⅛ teaspoon fine salt

Buttermilk Ice Cream (page 121) or vanilla ice cream, for serving

Roll, pan, and flute the dough as directed on pages 20–23. Transfer the pan to the refrigerator and chill the crust while you make the crumb and the filling.

Prepare the crumb as directed on page 85 and set it in the refrigerator to chill while you make the filling.

Preheat the oven to 375°F (190°C) with a rack in the center. Line a rimmed baking sheet with parchment paper.

In a large bowl, toss the cherries with the lemon juice and almond extract.

In a small bowl, whisk together the sugar, cornstarch, ground tapioca, and salt. Sprinkle the sugar mixture over the cherries and toss to coat. The mixture may seem dry at first; let it sit 10 minutes, and the lemon and sugar will draw more of the juices out of the fruit. Then give the mixture another good tossing to thoroughly moisten all of the sugar and tapioca granules.

Retrieve the prepared piecrust from the refrigerator and set the pan on the parchment-lined baking sheet. Pour the filling into the shell and top with the almond crumb, spreading evenly and covering all of the fruit.

Transfer the baking sheet to the oven and bake the pie 25 minutes, then rotate the baking sheet, lower the oven temperature to 350°F (175°C), and bake 25 to 30 minutes more, or until the juices bubble up through the crumb. Tent the top with foil if the crumb or crust starts to over-brown.

Transfer the pan to a wire rack and let the pie cool and set uncovered, at room temperature, overnight (or up to 3 days), before slicing and serving with ice cream.

almond crumb

Naturally sweet and buttery, almond pairs nicely with many fruits but plays especially well with cherries, peaches, apricots, and plums, all of which are its botanical cousins.

MAKES ABOUT 2 CUPS; ENOUGH TO TOP 1 (9-inch / 23-cm) PIE OR 12 (2-inch / 8-cm) MINI PIES

½ cup / 40 g rolled oats

½ cup / 62 g all-purpose flour

½ cup / 96 g granulated sugar

½ teaspoon ground cinnamon

¼ teaspoon fine salt

6 tablespoons / 85 g unsalted butter, melted and cooled

1 teaspoon freshly grated lemon zest

½ cup / 35 g sliced almonds

Use a food processor to grind the oats, pulsing the machine until the oats resemble coarse cornmeal.

Whisk the ground oats, flour, sugar, cinnamon, and salt together in a medium bowl. Add the melted butter and lemon zest and blend with your fingers or a fork until the butter is incorporated and the mixture gathers into small clumps. Add the almonds and toss gently. Chill the crumb 15 minutes before using for pie topping. (Can be made ahead and stored in an airtight container in the refrigerator for up to 1 week.)

apricot cherry oatmeal crumb pie

How serendipitous that apricots and sweet cherries come into season at the same time, smack in the middle of summer. As delicious as each of these fruits is solo, eaten straight out of hand, pairing and baking them unleashes a different sort of lusciousness altogether, and it's a wonderful way to revel in a fleeting moment.

MAKES 1 (9-inch / 23-cm) PIE

½ recipe Magpie Dough for Flaky Piecrust (page 17), chilled overnight

Oatmeal Crumb (page 57), substituting ground cinnamon for ground ginger

1 pound / 453 g ripe but firm apricots, halved and pitted, each half cut into thirds (small apricots) or quarters (large apricots)

1 pound / 453 g sweet cherries, pitted and halved

1 tablespoon freshly squeezed lemon juice

1 teaspoon vanilla extract

½ cup / 96 g granulated sugar

3 tablespoons finely ground instant tapioca (see page 45)

1 tablespoon cornstarch

Pinch fine salt

Ginger Ice Cream (page 123), for serving

Roll, pan, and flute the dough as directed on pages 20–23. Transfer the pan to the refrigerator and chill the shell while you make the crumb and the filling.

Prepare the crumb as directed on page 57 , using ground cinnamon instead of ground ginger. Transfer the bowl to the refrigerator and chill the crumb while you make the filling.

Preheat the oven to 375°F (190°C) with a rack in the center. Line a rimmed baking sheet with parchment paper.

In a large bowl, toss the apricots and cherries with the lemon juice and vanilla extract.

In a small bowl, whisk together the sugar, ground tapioca, cornstarch, and salt. Sprinkle the sugar mixture over the apricots and cherries and toss to coat. The mixture may seem dry at first; let it sit 10 minutes, and the lemon and sugar will draw the juices out of the fruit. Then give the mixture another good tossing to thoroughly moisten all of the sugar and tapioca granules.

Retrieve the piecrust and oatmeal crumb from the refrigerator. Set the pan on the parchment-lined baking sheet. Pour the filling into the pie shell. Top with oatmeal crumb, spreading evenly and covering all of the fruit.

Transfer the baking sheet to the oven and bake 25 minutes, then lower the oven temperature to 350°F (175°C) and bake 25 to 30 minutes more, or until the juices bubble up through the crumb. Tent the top with foil if the crumb or crust starts to over-brown.

Transfer the baking sheet to a wire rack and let the pie cool and set, uncovered, at room temperature, overnight (or up to 3 days) before slicing and serving with ginger ice cream.

blueberry cardamom pie with polenta streusel

Cardamom has a warm and sweet aroma with a complex bouquet of lemon, mint, black pepper, and floral notes—beautifully complementary to the sweet-tart summer flavor of blueberries. Grated apple, with its abundant pectin, serves as a natural thickener.

MAKES 1 (9-inch / 23-cm) PIE

½ recipe Magpie Dough for Flaky Piecrust (page 17), chilled overnight

Polenta Streusel (page 90)

1 Granny Smith apple

1 teaspoon freshly grated lemon zest

2 teaspoons freshly squeezed lemon juice

2 pounds / 907 g (about 2½ dry pints) blueberries

¾ cup / 144 g granulated sugar

2 tablespoons cornstarch

¼ teaspoon ground cardamom

⅛ teaspoon fine salt

Buttermilk Ice Cream (page 121) or Maple Bourbon Ice Cream (page 124), for serving

Roll, pan, and flute the dough as directed on pages 20–23. Transfer the pan to the refrigerator and chill the shell while you make the filling and the streusel.

Prepare the streusel as directed on page 90. Transfer the bowl to the refrigerator and chill the streusel while you make the filling.

Preheat the oven to 375°F (190°C) with a rack in the center. Line a baking sheet with parchment paper.

Peel the apple. Discard the peel. Line a large bowl with a clean, dry kitchen towel. Finely grate the apple flesh onto the towel, discarding the core. Wring the flesh dry with the towel and transfer back to the bowl. Add the zest and juice and toss to mix. Add the blueberries and toss to combine.

Whisk the sugar, cornstarch, cardamom, and salt together in a small bowl. Sprinkle the sugar mixture over the berries and toss to coat the fruit and moisten the sugar and cornstarch so that no dry white streaks remain.

Set the prepared pie shell on the parchment-lined baking sheet. Pour the filling into the shell, spreading evenly. Crumble the chilled streusel mixture on top of the filling, distributing it in an even layer and covering all of the fruit.

(Continued)

Transfer the baking sheet to the oven and bake the pie 25 minutes, then rotate the baking sheet, reduce the oven temperature to 350°F (175°C), and bake 30 minutes more, or until the juices bubble up through the streusel. Tent the top of the pie with foil if the streusel or crust begins to over-brown.

Let the pie cool and set uncovered, at room temperature, overnight (or up to 3 days) before slicing and serving with buttermilk or maple bourbon ice cream.

polenta streusel

Take that perfectly sweet and crusty half-inch off the top of the very best corn muffin you ever had, add a warm hint of cardamom-ginger spice, and you've got this crumb: so tasty.

MAKES ABOUT 2 CUPS; ENOUGH TO TOP 1 (9-inch / 23-cm) PIE OR 12 (2-inch / 8-cm) MINI PIES

½ cup / 96 g granulated sugar

1 teaspoon freshly grated lemon zest

1 teaspoon ground cardamom

½ teaspoon ground ginger

1¼ cups / 150 g all-purpose flour

¾ cup / 125 g polenta (fine yellow cornmeal)

1 teaspoon baking powder

½ teaspoon fine salt

½ cup / 113 g cold unsalted butter, cut into ½-inch cubes

1 large egg, lightly beaten

Combine the sugar and lemon zest in a medium bowl and mix until the sugar looks damp and starts to clump a bit. Add the cardamom, ginger, flour, polenta, baking powder, and salt and whisk until well combined. Add the butter cubes and blend with your fingers or a fork until the mixture resembles coarse crumbs. Drizzle in the egg and stir the mixture with a fork until it is evenly moistened and begins to gather into small clumps. Set the bowl in the refrigerator and chill the streusel for 15 minutes before topping your pie.

blueberry rhuby rose pie

The combination of blueberries and rhubarb and a splash of rosewater makes a violet-blue pie that looks and tastes amazing.

◄ MAKES 1 (9-inch / 23-cm) PIE ►

1 recipe Magpie Dough for Flaky Piecrust (page 17), chilled overnight

1 pound / 453 g blueberries

1 pound / 453 g rhubarb, trimmed and cut into ½-inch pieces

2 teaspoons freshly squeezed lemon juice

2 teaspoons vanilla extract

1 teaspoon rosewater (optional)

1 cup / 192 g granulated sugar

1 tablespoon cornstarch

¼ cup / 48 g finely ground instant tapioca (see page 45)

⅛ teaspoon fine salt

1 large egg yolk

2 tablespoons sanding sugar or coarse raw sugar (optional), for sprinkling

Ginger Ice Cream (page 123) or vanilla ice cream, for serving

Follow the instructions on page 27 to roll and pan the dough for the top and bottom crust. Transfer the pans to the refrigerator to chill the dough while you make the filling.

Preheat the oven to 400°F (200°C) with a rack in the center. Line a rimmed baking sheet with parchment paper.

In a large bowl, toss the blueberries and rhubarb with the lemon juice, vanilla, and rosewater, if using.

In a small bowl, whisk together the sugar, cornstarch, tapioca, and salt. Sprinkle the sugar mixture over the fruit and toss to coat. Let it sit 10 minutes, then give the mixture another good tossing to thoroughly moisten all of the sugar and tapioca granules.

(Continued)

Retrieve the prepared bottom crust from the refrigerator. Set the pan on the parchment-lined baking sheet and pour the filling into the shell. Use your index finger to scrape some of the syrupy fruit juices off the sides of the mixing bowl and generously moisten the top edge of the shell.

Fetch the prepared top crust from the refrigerator and follow the instructions on page 27 to transfer the sheet of dough to the top of the pie and trim the edges. Gently pinch the edges of the dough together, folding under and tucking securely inside the lip of the pan.

In a small bowl, whisk the egg yolk with 1 tablespoon water. Lightly brush the top of the pie with the egg wash and sprinkle with the sanding sugar. Use a small, sharp knife or kitchen shears to cut 4 slits, each about 2 inches long, toward the center of the dough.

Transfer the baking sheet to the oven and bake the pie 25 minutes, then rotate the baking sheet, lower the oven temperature to 350°F (175°C), and bake 25 to 30 minutes more, or until the juices bubble up through the vent holes. Tent the top with foil if the crust starts to over-brown.

Transfer the baking sheet to a wire rack and let the pie cool and set uncovered, at room temperature, overnight (or up to 3 days) before slicing and serving with ginger or vanilla ice cream.

peach lattice pie with bourbon caramel

Peach lattice is a beautifully classic summer pie. A drizzling of rich, buttery bourbon caramel over each slice heightens the naturally lush sweetness of ripe peaches—ditto a scoop of ginger ice cream on the side.

MAKES 1 (9-inch / 23-cm) PIE

1 recipe Magpie Dough for Flaky Piecrust (page 17), chilled overnight

2 pounds / 907 g ripe peaches, each peeled, halved, pitted, and cut into 8 wedges

½ cup / 96 g packed light brown sugar

1 tablespoon vanilla extract

1 tablespoon freshly squeezed lemon juice

½ cup / 96 g granulated sugar

3 tablespoons finely ground instant tapioca (see page 45)

½ teaspoon ground cinnamon

⅛ teaspoon fine salt

1 large egg yolk

2 tablespoons sanding sugar or coarse raw sugar, for sprinkling

Bourbon Caramel Sauce (page 96), for serving

Ginger Ice Cream (page 123), for serving

Roll and pan the dough for the bottom crust as directed on page 29; follow the instructions to roll and cut 1-inch-wide lattice strips for the top of the pie. Transfer the pans to the refrigerator and chill the dough while you make the filling.

Preheat the oven to 400°F (200°C) with a rack in the center. Line a rimmed baking sheet with parchment paper.

In a large bowl, toss the peaches with the brown sugar, vanilla extract, and lemon juice. Let sit 5 minutes.

In a small bowl, whisk together the granulated sugar, ground tapioca, cinnamon, and salt. Sprinkle the sugar mixture over the peaches

(Continued)

and toss to combine. The mixture may look dry at first; let it sit at room temperature for 10 to 15 minutes to allow the sugar and lemon juice to draw more of the juices out of the fruit, then give it another good tossing to mix well and moisten all of the sugar and tapioca granules.

Retrieve the prepared crust from the refrigerator and set the pan on the parchment-lined baking sheet. Pour the filling into the bottom shell. Use your index finger to scrape some of the syrupy fruit juices off the sides of the mixing bowl and generously moisten the top edge of the shell.

Follow the instructions on pages 29–31 to lattice the top with the dough strips and roll and crimp the edges.

Whisk the egg yolk with 1 tablespoon water. Lightly brush the lattice with the egg wash and sprinkle with sanding sugar. Transfer the baking sheet to the oven and bake the pie 25 minutes, then rotate the baking sheet, lower the oven temperature to 350°F (175°C), and bake 30 minutes more, or until the juices bubble up through the lattice. Tent the top with foil if the crust starts to over-brown.

Set the baking sheet on a wire rack and let the pie cool and set uncovered, at room temperature, overnight (or up to 3 days) before slicing and serving. Serve with bourbon caramel sauce and ginger ice cream.

bourbon caramel sauce

See page 49 if you need a non-boozy caramel sauce. Don't hesitate to serve both options!

MAKES 1½ CUPS

2 cups / 400 g granulated sugar

¾ cup / 170 g unsalted butter

1¼ cups / 295 g heavy cream,
at room temperature

1 teaspoon kosher salt

3 teaspoons vanilla extract

2 tablespoons bourbon

Pour the sugar into a medium high-sided saucepan, tilting the pan to distribute the sugar evenly across the bottom of the pan. Set the pan over medium-high heat. Use a rubber spatula to occasionally push the sugar from the outer edge of the pan toward the center. The sugar will clump up slightly, but just keep pushing it around a bit; it will eventually smooth out. When the sugar is dissolved and darkened to the color of a copper penny (about 5 to 7 minutes), add the butter and whisk until incorporated. Be careful: the mixture will bubble up when you add the butter and might even seem like it's about to overflow the pan; just keep whisking and it will quickly settle back down.

Take the pan off the heat and carefully add the cream in two stages, whisking until smooth and incorporated. Add the salt, vanilla, and bourbon, whisking to combine.

Pour the caramel through a fine-mesh strainer into a bowl and cool completely to room temperature, about 2 hours, before using or transferring to an airtight container to store in the refrigerator. Return to room temperature before using.

raspberry rhubarb pie

Sweet raspberries pair well with tart rhubarb, and the two combine into a beautiful ruby-red filling. Vanilla bean scrapings add a creamy smoothness to the mix.

◄ MAKES 1 (9-inch / 23-cm) PIE ►

1 recipe Magpie Dough for Flaky Piecrust (page 17), chilled overnight

1½ pounds / 680 g rhubarb, trimmed and coarsely chopped

8 ounces fresh or frozen raspberries

2 teaspoons freshly squeezed lemon juice

1 teaspoon vanilla extract

1 cup / 192 g granulated sugar

¼ cup / 48 g finely ground instant tapioca (see page 45)

1 tablespoon plus 1 teaspoon cornstarch

⅛ teaspoon fine salt

⅓ vanilla bean

1 large egg yolk

2 tablespoons sanding sugar or coarse raw sugar, for sprinkling

Ginger Ice Cream (page 123) or Buttermilk Ice Cream (page 121), for serving

Follow the instructions on page 27 to roll and pan the bottom crust and the sheet of dough for the top crust. Transfer the pan and the baking sheet to the refrigerator to chill the dough while you make the filling.

Preheat the oven to 400°F (200°C) with a rack in the center. Line a rimmed baking sheet with parchment paper.

In a large bowl, toss the rhubarb and raspberries with the lemon juice and vanilla.

In a small bowl, whisk together the granulated sugar, ground tapioca, cornstarch, and salt. Use a small, sharp knife to split the vanilla bean lengthwise and scrape the sticky seeds into the bowl, whisking to incorporate.

(Continued)

Sprinkle the sugar mixture over the fruit and toss to combine. The mixture may seem dry at first; let it sit 10 to 15 minutes, and the lemon and sugar will draw the juices out of the fruit. Then give the mixture another good tossing to thoroughly moisten all of the sugar and tapioca granules.

Retrieve the prepared bottom crust from the refrigerator. Set the pan on the parchment-lined baking sheet and pour the filling into the pie shell. Use your index finger to scrape some of the syrupy fruit juices off the sides of the mixing bowl and generously moisten the top edge of the shell.

Fetch the top crust from the refrigerator and follow the instructions on pages 27–28 to transfer the sheet of dough to the top of the pie and trim and tuck the edges.

Whisk the egg yolk with 1 tablespoon water. Lightly brush the crust with the egg wash and sprinkle with the sanding sugar. If you didn't cut decorative vent holes in the top crust before transferring it to the pie, use kitchen shears or a small sharp knife to cut four 2-inch-long slits near the center.

Transfer the baking sheet to the oven and bake the pie 25 minutes, then rotate the baking sheet, lower the oven temperature to 350°F (175°C), and bake 25 to 30 minutes more, or until the juices bubble up through the vent holes. Tent the top with foil if it starts to over-brown.

Transfer the baking sheet to a wire rack and let the pie cool and set uncovered, at room temperature, overnight (or up to 3 days), before slicing and serving. Serve with buttermilk or ginger ice cream.

raspberry mini pies with white chocolate crumb

Little pies filled with succulent raspberries and topped with rich white chocolate crumb are a superb treat any time of year. If you are using frozen raspberries, be sure to thaw them partway; they need to be juicy to dissolve the sugar and cornstarch mixture that thickens the filling just right.

MAKES 12 (3-inch / 8-cm) MINI PIES

1 recipe Magpie Dough for Flaky Piecrust (page 17), chilled overnight

White Chocolate Crumb (page 101)

1 pound / 453 g fresh or frozen and partially thawed raspberries

2 teaspoons freshly squeezed lemon juice

1 teaspoon vanilla extract

½ cup / 96 g granulated sugar

1 tablespoon cornstarch

Pinch fine salt

Follow the directions on page 32 to roll, cut, and pan the dough for mini pies. Transfer the muffin tin to the refrigerator and chill the shells while you make the filling and the crumb.

Prepare the crumb as directed on page 101. Transfer the bowl to the refrigerator to chill while you make the filling.

Preheat the oven to 375°F (190°C) with a rack in the center. Line a baking sheet with parchment paper.

In a large bowl, toss the raspberries with the lemon juice and vanilla.

In a small bowl, whisk together the sugar, cornstarch, and salt. Sprinkle the sugar mixture over the berries and toss well to coat the berries and thoroughly moisten the cornstarch and sugar so that no dry white streaks remain.

Retrieve the pan from the refrigerator and set it on the parchment-lined baking sheet. Distribute the raspberry mixture evenly among the shells. Divide the white chocolate crumb among the tops of the pies, spreading evenly and covering all of the fruit.

(Continued)

Transfer the baking sheet to the oven and bake the pies 20 to 25 minutes, or until the crumb is golden and the juice bubbles up through the topping.

Set the pan on a wire rack and let the pies cool to room temperature before using a butter knife to carefully lift out each pie.

white chocolate crumb

We created this decadent crumb especially for our mini raspberry pies. It would also be great on a strawberry, blueberry, or blackberry pie.

MAKES ABOUT 2 CUPS; ENOUGH TO TOP 12 (3-inch / 8-cm) MINI PIES OR 1 (9-inch / 23-cm) PIE

½ cup / 40 g rolled oats

½ cup / 62 g all-purpose flour

½ cup / 96 g granulated sugar

½ teaspoon ground cinnamon

¼ teaspoon fine salt

6 tablespoons / 85 g unsalted butter, melted and cooled

½ cup / 88 g white chocolate chips

Use a food processor to grind the oats, pulsing the machine until the oats resemble coarse cornmeal.

Whisk the ground oats, flour, sugar, cinnamon, and salt together in a medium bowl. Add the melted butter and blend with your fingers or a fork until the butter is incorporated and the mixture gathers into small clumps. Add the white chocolate chips and toss gently to mix. Chill the crumb for 5 to 10 minutes before using for topping.

peach raspberry orange blossom pie

This is simply the prettiest pie to behold and to savor.

⟨ MAKES 1 (9-inch / 23-cm) PIE ⟩

½ recipe Magpie Dough for Flaky Piecrust (page 17), chilled overnight

Cinnamon Crumb (page 103)

2 pounds ripe peaches, each peeled, halved, pitted, and cut into 8 wedges

½ dry pint / 170 g fresh raspberries

1 tablespoon freshly grated orange zest

1 tablespoon freshly squeezed orange juice

1½ teaspoons orange blossom water

1¼ cups / 240 g granulated sugar

3 tablespoons finely ground instant tapioca (see page 45)

1 tablespoon cornstarch

⅛ teaspoon fine salt

Ginger Ice Cream (page 123) or vanilla ice cream, for serving

Roll, pan, trim, and flute the dough as directed on pages 20–23. Transfer the pan to the refrigerator and chill the shell while you make the filling and the crumb.

Prepare the crumb according to the recipe on page 103 and set it in the refrigerator to chill while you make the filling.

Preheat the oven to 375°F (190°C) with a rack in the center. Line a baking sheet with parchment paper.

In a large bowl, toss the peaches and raspberries with the orange zest, orange juice, and orange blossom water.

In a small bowl, whisk together the sugar, ground tapioca, cornstarch, and salt. Sprinkle the sugar mixture over the fruit and toss to combine. The mixture may seem dry at first; set the bowl aside at room temperature for 10 to 15 minutes, or until the fruits release more of their juices. Then give the mixture another good tossing to thoroughly moisten all of the sugar and tapioca granules.

Retrieve the prepared crust and the cinnamon crumb from the refrigerator. Set the pie pan on the baking sheet and pour the filling into the crust. Top the pie with the crumb, spreading evenly and covering all of the fruit.

Transfer the baking sheet to the oven and bake the pie 25 minutes, then rotate the sheet, lower the oven temperature to 350°F (175°C), and bake 25 to 30 minutes more, or until the juices bubble up through the crumb. Tent the top with foil if the crumb starts to over-brown.

Transfer the baking sheet to a wire rack and let the pie cool and set uncovered, at room temperature, overnight (or up to 3 days), before slicing and serving. Serve with ginger or vanilla ice cream.

cinnamon crumb

You could add chopped walnuts or pecans to this delicate crumb, if you'd like.

MAKES ABOUT 2 CUPS; ENOUGH TO TOP 1 (9-inch / 23-cm) PIE OR 12 (3-inch / 8-cm) MINI PIES

1⅓ cups / 165 g all-purpose flour

⅔ cup / 128 g granulated sugar

1 teaspoon ground cinnamon

¾ teaspoon baking powder

¼ teaspoon fine salt

½ cup / 113 g unsalted butter, melted and cooled

Whisk the flour, sugar, cinnamon, baking powder, and salt together in a medium bowl. Add the melted butter and blend with your fingers or a fork until the butter is incorporated and the mixture gathers into small clumps. Chill for 5 to 10 minutes before using as pie topping.

berry lavender crumb pie

Ripening times for summer and fall berries synch up nicely with lavender bloom times, so you can use freshly picked and dried lavender if you like. Either way, the flavor combination is marvelous.

MAKES 1 (9-inch / 23-cm) PIE

½ recipe Magpie Dough for Flaky Piecrust (page 17), chilled overnight

Lavendar Crumb (page 106)

1 Granny Smith apple

2 pounds mixed berries (raspberries, blueberries, blackberries)

2 teaspoons freshly squeezed lemon juice

2 teaspoons vanilla extract

¾ cup / 144 g granulated sugar

2 tablespoons cornstarch

1 tablespoon finely ground instant tapioca (see page 45)

⅛ teaspoon fine salt

Ginger Ice Cream (page 123) or vanilla ice cream, for serving

Follow the instructions on pages 20–23 to roll, pan, and flute the crust. Transfer the pan to the refrigerator and chill the shell while you make the crumb and the filling.

Prepare the crumb according to the instructions on page 106. Transfer to the refrigerator to chill while you make the filling.

Preheat the oven to 375°F (190°C) with a rack in the center. Line a baking sheet with parchment paper.

Peel the apple. Discard the peel. Line a large bowl with a clean, dry kitchen towel. Finely grate the apple flesh onto the towel, discarding the core. Wring the apple flesh dry with the towel and transfer the grated flesh back to the bowl. Add the berries, lemon juice, and vanilla extract and mix to combine.

Whisk the sugar, cornstarch, ground tapioca, and salt together in a small bowl. Sprinkle the sugar mixture over the berries and toss to combine. Set the bowl aside at room temperature for 10 to 15 minutes, or until the berries start to release their juices. Then give the mixture another good tossing to thoroughly moisten all of the sugar and tapioca granules.

Retrieve the pie shell and the lavender crumb from the refrigerator. Set the pan on the parchment-lined baking sheet. Pour the filling into the shell and evenly spread the crumb, covering all of the fruit. Transfer the baking

(Continued)

sheet to the oven and bake the pie 25 minutes, then rotate the sheet, lower the oven temperature to 350°F (175°C), and bake another 25 to 30 minutes, or until the juices bubble up through the crumb. Tent the top with foil if the crumb starts to over-brown.

Set the baking sheet on a wire rack and let the pie cool, uncovered and at room temperature, overnight (or up to 3 days) before slicing and serving. Serve with ginger or vanilla ice cream.

lavender crumb

The flavor and fragrance of the lavender in this crumb is very subtle and delicate—a faint floral whisper with a chocolate undertone. Combined with nutty oats, a little sweetness from the sugar, and the bright zing of lemon zest, it all adds up to complement berries beautifully.

MAKES ABOUT 2 CUPS; ENOUGH TO TOP 1 (9-inch / 23-cm) PIE OR 12 (3-inch / 8-cm) MINI PIES

½ cup / 40 g rolled oats

½ cup / 62 g all-purpose flour

½ cup / 96 g granulated sugar

1 teaspoon freshly grated lemon zest

¼ teaspoon fine salt

1 teaspoon dried lavender buds

6 tablespoons / 85 g unsalted butter, melted and cooled

Use a food processor to grind the oats, pulsing the machine until the oats resemble coarse cornmeal.

Whisk the ground oats, flour, sugar, lemon zest, and salt together in a medium bowl. Sprinkle in the lavender, rubbing the flowers between your fingers to break them apart a bit. Add the melted butter and blend with your fingers or a fork until the butter is incorporated and the mixture gathers into small clumps. Transfer the bowl to the refrigerator and chill 5 to 10 minutes before using for pie topping.

berry custard thyme crumb pie

Creamy custard, fresh berries, and a delicate dusting of thyme crumb make this is a wonderful pie to serve to company or take to a party.

◆ **MAKES 1 (9-inch / 23-cm) PIE** ◆

½ recipe Magpie Dough for Flaky Piecrust (page 17), chilled overnight

Thyme Crumb (page 109)

1 cup / 192 g granulated sugar

¼ cup / 31 g all-purpose flour

½ vanilla bean

2 large eggs

½ cup / 115 g sour cream

1 teaspoon vanilla extract

1 teaspoon freshly grated lemon zest

2 teaspoons freshly squeezed lemon juice

⅛ teaspoon fine salt

½ dry pint / 88 g fresh blackberries

½ dry pint / 88 g fresh raspberries

Lightly sweetened freshly whipped cream, for serving

Follow the instructions on pages 20–24 to roll, pan, trim, flute, and parbake the crust. Set the pan on a wire rack and cool the shell to room temperature while you make the crumb and the filling.

Prepare the crumb as directed on page 109 and set the bowl in the refrigerator to chill while you make the filling.

Preheat the oven to 350°F (175°C) with a rack in the center. Line a baking sheet with parchment paper.

To make the custard filling, whisk the sugar and flour together in a large bowl. Use a small sharp knife to split the vanilla bean lengthwise and scrape the sticky seeds into the bowl, whisking to combine.

In a medium bowl, whisk the eggs, sour cream, and vanilla together. Add the lemon zest, lemon juice, and salt and mix well. Pour the egg mixture into the bowl with the flour mixture and whisk until smooth and uniformly combined.

Set the prepared shell on the parchment-lined baking sheet and spread the berries evenly across the bottom. Pour the custard over the berries and

(Continued)

scatter the thyme crumb over top. Carefully transfer the baking sheet to the oven and bake the pie for 30 to 40 minutes, rotating halfway through the baking time, until the top is golden brown and the custard is set at the edges but still slightly jiggly in the middle.

Set the baking sheet on a wire rack and let the pie cool completely to room temperature. Cover with plastic wrap and transfer to the refrigerator to chill overnight (at least 12 hours and up to 3 days) before slicing and serving with whipped cream.

spin

Vanilla Crème Brûlée Pie: *Leave out the berries and skip the thyme crumb. After the vanilla custard has baked and set overnight, sprinkle with coarse raw sugar and use a kitchen torch to caramelize the sugar. Let cool to allow the sugar to harden before serving.*

thyme crumb

The idea of thyme crumb on a sweet berry pie has raised many a skeptical eyebrow in the shop, but one bite is all it takes to convince just about anyone that it's a very good thing. The thyme flavor and aroma are very subtle and don't take the pie in a savory direction. It's most definitely dessert.

MAKES ABOUT ½ CUP; ENOUGH TO TOP 1 (9-inch / 23-cm) PIE

¼ cup / 31 g all-purpose flour

¼ cup / 48 g packed light brown sugar

1 teaspoon ground ginger

⅛ teaspoon ground or freshly grated nutmeg

½ teaspoon finely chopped fresh thyme leaves

¼ teaspoon fine salt

3 tablespoons unsalted butter, melted and cooled

Whisk the flour, brown sugar, ginger, nutmeg, thyme, and salt together in a small bowl. Pour in the butter and blend with your fingers or a fork until the mixture gathers into small clumps. Transfer the bowl to the refrigerator and chill 5 to 10 minutes before using for pie topping.

apricot rosemary crumb pie

Apricot pie is pure summer joy. Rosemary crumb topping brings a faint whiff of exotic fragrance to the lush, full-bodied sweetness of the fruit. Feel free to substitute Cinnamon Crumb (page 103).

⟨ MAKES 1 (9-inch / 23-cm) PIE ⟩

½ recipe Magpie Dough for Flaky Piecrust (page 17), chilled overnight

Rosemary Crumb (page 111)

1 pound ripe apricots, pitted and halved, each half cut into 3 wedges

1 tablespoon freshly squeezed lemon juice

1 teaspoon vanilla extract

¾ cup / 144 g granulated sugar

3 tablespoons finely ground instant tapioca (see page 45)

1 teaspoon cornstarch

Pinch fine salt

Maple Bourbon Ice Cream (page 124), for serving

Lightly sweetened freshly whipped cream, for serving

Follow the instructions on pages 20–23 to roll, pan, and flute the crust. Transfer the shell to the refrigerator to chill while you prepare the crumb and the filling.

Prepare the rosemary crumb as directed on page 111. Set the bowl in the refrigerator and chill the crumb while you make the filling.

Preheat the oven to 375°F (190°C) with a rack in the center. Line a rimmed baking sheet with parchment paper.

In a large bowl, toss the apricots with the lemon juice and vanilla extract.

In a small bowl, whisk together the sugar, ground tapioca, cornstarch, and salt. Sprinkle the sugar mixture over the apricots and toss to coat. The mixture may look dry at first; let it sit at room temperature for 10 to 15 minutes to allow the sugar and lemon juice to draw the juices out of the fruit, then give it another good tossing to mix well and moisten all of the sugar and tapioca granules.

Retrieve the pie shell from the refrigerator and set the pan on the prepared baking sheet. Pour the filling into the shell, spreading evenly. Fetch the crumb from the refrigerator and spread evenly on top of the filling, covering all of the fruit.

Transfer the baking sheet to the oven and bake the pie 25 minutes, then rotate the baking sheet, lower the oven temperature to 350°F (175°C), and bake 25 to 30 minutes more, or until the juices bubble up through the crumb. Tent the top with foil if the crumb or crust starts to over-brown.

Transfer the baking sheet to a wire rack and let the pie cool and set uncovered, at room temperature, overnight (or up to 3 days), before slicing and serving.

Serve with maple bourbon ice cream and whipped cream.

rosemary crumb

We developed this crumb to grace apricot pie; it also makes a terrific topping for apple pie.

MAKES ABOUT 2 CUPS; ENOUGH TO TOP 1 (9-inch / 23-cm) PIE

½ cup / 40 g rolled oats

½ cup / 62 g all-purpose flour

½ cup / 96 g packed light brown sugar

½ teaspoon ground cinnamon

¼ teaspoon fine salt

1 teaspoon finely chopped fresh rosemary leaves

6 tablespoons / 85 g unsalted butter, at room temperature

Use a food processor to grind the oats, pulsing the machine until the oats resemble coarse cornmeal. Add the flour, sugar, cinnamon, and salt and pulse 5 times to combine.

Transfer the mixture to a medium bowl and whisk in the rosemary. Add the butter and blend with your hands or a fork until the butter is incorporated and the mixture gathers into small clumps. Chill 5 to 10 minutes before topping pie.

wild blackberry lattice-top pie

Farmstand or true wild blackberries are the way to go for this pie; commercially grown varieties available in supermarkets lack that true, deeply dark sweet blackberry flavor.

◀ **MAKES 1 (9-inch / 23-cm) PIE** ▶

1 recipe Magpie Dough for Flaky Piecrust (page 17), chilled overnight

2 pounds wild blackberries

2 teaspoons freshly squeezed lemon juice

1 teaspoon vanilla extract

¾ cup /144 g granulated sugar

3 tablespoons finely ground instant tapioca (see page 45)

1 tablespoon cornstarch

½ teaspoon ground ginger

⅛ teaspoon fine salt

1 large egg yolk

2 tablespoons sanding sugar or coarse raw sugar, for sprinkling

Ginger Ice Cream (page 123), for serving

Roll and pan the dough for the bottom crust as directed on page 29; follow the instructions to roll and cut 1-inch-wide strips for the top of the pie. Transfer the pans to the refrigerator and chill the dough while you make the filling.

Preheat the oven to 400°F (200°C) with a rack in the center. Line a baking sheet with parchment paper.

In a large bowl, toss the blackberries with the lemon juice and vanilla extract.

In a small bowl, whisk together the granulated sugar, ground tapioca, cornstarch, ginger, and salt. Sprinkle the sugar mixture over the blackberries and toss to coat. The mixture may look dry at first; let it sit at room temperature for 10 to 15 minutes to allow the sugar and lemon juice to draw the juices out of the fruit, then give it a good tossing to mix well and moisten all of the sugar and tapioca granules.

Retrieve the prepared bottom crust from the refrigerator and set it on the parchment-lined baking sheet. Pour the filling into the shell. Use your index finger to scrape some of the syrupy fruit juices off the sides of the mixing bowl and generously moisten the top edge of the shell.

Fetch the dough strips from the refrigerator and follow the instructions on pages 29–31 to lattice the top of the pie and trim, tuck, and crimp the edge.

Whisk the egg yolk with 1 tablespoon water. Lightly brush the lattice with the egg wash and sprinkle with the sanding sugar.

Transfer the baking sheet to the oven, bake the pie 25 minutes, then reduce the oven temperature to 350°F (175°C) and bake 25 to 30 minutes more, or until the juices bubble up through the lattice. Tent the top with foil if the crust starts to over-brown.

Transfer the baking sheet to a wire rack and let the pie cool and set, uncovered, at room temperature, overnight (or up to 3 days) before slicing and serving with ginger ice cream.

blackberry bourbon pie with lavender cream

Deep purple pleasure in a pie shell, this is a cupboard pie you can make any time of year. The pectin and sugar in the jam (not jelly, and not fruit spread!) enhance the custard-like structure of the filling. Feel free to serve topped with fresh blackberries as well as the lavender cream.

◆ MAKES 1 (9-inch / 23-cm) PIE ◆

½ recipe Magpie Dough for Flaky Piecrust (page 17), chilled overnight

½ cup / 96 g granulated sugar

1 tablespoon cornstarch

⅛ teaspoon fine salt

1 (10-ounce / 283 g) jar seedless blackberry jam

4 large eggs

2 tablespoons unsalted butter, melted and cooled

1 teaspoon vanilla extract

1 teaspoon freshly grated lemon zest

2 tablespoons bourbon

Lavender Cream (page 115), for serving

Follow the instructions on pages 20–24 to roll, pan, flute, and parbake the crust. Set the pan on a wire rack and let the shell cool to room temperature while you make the filling.

In a large bowl, whisk together the sugar, cornstarch, and salt until well blended. Add the jam and eggs and whisk until smooth, then whisk in the melted butter, vanilla, zest, and bourbon and continue whisking until fully combined and smooth. Set the mixture aside for 10 minutes.

Preheat the oven to 350°F (175°C) with a rack in the center. Line a rimmed baking sheet with parchment paper. Set the parbaked piecrust on the parchment-lined baking sheet.

Stir the filling with a whisk, pour it into the shell, and bake the pie 25 minutes, or until the sides are set but the center is slightly jiggly, rotating halfway through the baking time.

Transfer the baking sheet to a wire rack and let the pie cool to room temperature, then cover with plastic wrap and chill overnight (at least 12 hours or up to 3 days) before slicing and serving. Serve with a generous dollop of lavender cream atop each slice.

lavender cream

This ethereal cream is lovely with any simple fruit dessert.

◀◼ MAKES 2 CUPS ◼▶

1 cup / 237 ml heavy cream

2 tablespoons granulated sugar

2 teaspoons dried lavender buds

Combine the cream and sugar in a medium saucepan, set the pan over medium-high heat, and stir constantly until the mixture is steaming (don't boil!). Take the pan off the heat and gently stir in the lavender. Cover the pan and let the cream steep for 30 minutes.

Pour the infused cream through a fine-mesh strainer into a medium bowl and discard the lavender buds. Set the bowl in the refrigerator to chill the cream.

When the cream is thoroughly chilled, use an electric mixer at high speed to whip the cream to medium peaks. Use the lavender cream immediately or keep in an airtight container in the refrigerator for up to 3 days.

plum cherry almond crumb pie

This pie is a perfect way to savor summer while it lasts—ripe red plums and sweet cherries are a sure sign that the season of sultry fruit will soon draw to a close.

MAKES 1 (9-inch / 23-cm) PIE

½ recipe Magpie Dough for Flaky Piecrust (page 17), chilled overnight

Almond Crumb (page 85)

1½ pounds red plums, halved and pitted, each half cut into 4 wedges

6 ounces / 170 g sweet cherries, halved and pitted

1 teaspoon freshly squeezed lemon juice

1 teaspoon almond extract

½ cup / 96 g granulated sugar

3 tablespoons cornstarch

⅛ teaspoon fine salt

Lightly sweetened freshly whipped cream, for serving

Follow the directions on pages 20–23 to roll, pan, trim, and flute the dough. Transfer the pan to the refrigerator and chill the shell while you make the filling and the crumb. Prepare the crumb (page 85) and chill it in the refrigerator.

Preheat the oven to 375°F (190°C) with a rack in the center. Line a baking sheet with parchment paper.

In a large bowl, toss the plums and cherries with the lemon juice and almond extract.

In a small bowl, whisk together the sugar, cornstarch, and salt. Sprinkle it over the fruit and toss well, coating the fruit and thoroughly moistening the cornstarch and sugar.

Set the piecrust on the parchment-lined baking sheet. Pour the filling into the shell and top with the chilled almond crumb, spreading evenly and covering all of the fruit.

Transfer the baking sheet to the oven and bake the pie 25 minutes, then rotate the pie, lower the oven temperature to 350°F (175°C), and bake 25 to 30 minutes more, or until the juices bubble up through the crumb. Tent the top with foil if the crumb or the edges of the crust start to over-brown.

Transfer the baking sheet to a wire rack and let the pie cool and set, uncovered, at room temperature, overnight (or up to 3 days) before slicing and serving. Serve with whipped cream.

five-spice plum pie

We were delighted to discover that the juicy sweetness of plums is beautifully heightened by the heady aroma of Chinese five-spice powder (usually made of ground star anise, fennel, Szechuan pepper, clove, and cinnamon—and sometimes a bit of licorice root or ground ginger as well).

◄ MAKES 1 (9-inch / 23-cm) PIE ►

1 recipe Magpie Dough for Flaky Piecrust (page 17), chilled overnight

2 pounds / 906 g red plums, halved and pitted, each half cut into 4 wedges

1 teaspoon vanilla extract

1 teaspoon freshly squeezed lemon juice

½ cup / 96 g packed light brown sugar

½ teaspoon Chinese five-spice powder

½ teaspoon ground ginger

3 tablespoons cornstarch

⅛ teaspoon fine salt

1 large egg yolk

2 tablespoons sanding sugar or coarse raw sugar, for sprinkling

Maple Bourbon Ice Cream (page 124) or Ginger Ice Cream (page 123), for serving

Follow the instructions on page 27 to roll and pan the bottom crust and the sheet of dough for the top crust. Transfer the pan and the baking sheet to the refrigerator to chill the dough while you make the filling.

Preheat the oven to 400°F (200°C) with a rack in the center. Line a rimmed baking sheet with parchment paper.

To make the filling, in a large bowl, toss the plums with the vanilla and lemon juice.

In a small bowl, whisk together the brown sugar, spices, cornstarch, and salt. Sprinkle the brown sugar mixture over the plums and toss well to coat the fruit and thoroughly moisten the cornstarch and sugar so that no dry white streaks remain.

Retrieve the prepared bottom crust from the refrigerator. Set the pan on the parchment-lined baking sheet and pour the filling into the pie shell. Use your index finger to scrape some of the syrupy fruit juices off the sides of the mixing bowl and generously moisten the top edge of the shell.

Fetch the top crust from the refrigerator and follow the instructions on pages 27–28 to transfer the sheet of dough to the top of the pie and trim and tuck the edges. If you didn't cut decorative vent holes in the top crust before transferring it to the pie, use kitchen shears or a small sharp knife to cut four 2-inch-long slits near the center. Whisk the egg yolk with 1 tablespoon water. Lightly brush the top of the pie with the egg wash and sprinkle with sanding sugar.

Transfer the baking sheet to the oven and bake the pie 25 minutes, then rotate the baking sheet, lower the oven temperature to 350°F (175°C), and bake 25 to 30 minutes more, or until the juices bubble up through the vent holes. Tent the top with foil if it starts to over-brown.

Transfer the baking sheet to a wire rack and let the pie cool and set, uncovered, at room temperature, overnight (or up to 3 days) before slicing and serving. Serve with maple bourbon or ginger ice cream.

À LA MODE

Some pies want for just a dollop of lightly sweetened whipped cream; that's how I like tart lemony pies (page 71 and 73) and Roasted Sweet Potato Pie (page 142). Others, such as our Berry Custard with Thyme Crumb (page 107) and Butterscotch Bourbon (page 160) are best served naked. But for a great many pies, a scoop of ice cream is just the thing.

From the get-go at Magpie, it seemed only right to stock big tubs of vanilla ice cream from a local Philly maker, Bassett's. Then came the day I improvised an enormous batch of buttermilk ice cream as a sensible way of coping with a surprise surplus of the thick tangy stuff and added house-made buttermilk ice cream as an optional accompaniment to our spring sweet pie menu, which featured Raspberry Rhubarb (page 97) and Strawberry Crumb (page 79). The buttermilk ice cream went like gangbusters. Thus Magpie's tradition of small-batch house-made ice cream was born.

Other specialty Magpie-made ice creams are less accidental. Infused with fresh ginger root and dotted with candied ginger bits, our Ginger Ice Cream (page 123) was created for our summer menu, to accompany Blueberry Cardamom Pie with Polenta Streusel (page 88) and Peach Lattice Pie with Bourbon Caramel (page 93).

As a bourbon fan and a dessert purveyor, I take particular delight in our Maple Bourbon (page 124), an ice cream that brings together the innate caramel-tinged richness of both the syrup and the booze. It's perfect with autumnal numbers, like Apple Cranberry Walnut Lattice Pie (page 51), and wickedly delicious with Oatmeal Cookie Pie (page 150).

Making your own ice cream is as easy as whipping up a quick custard, chilling it down, chucking it in an ice cream maker for a spell, then freezing it overnight. It makes homemade pie even more special. Give it a try!

BUTTERMILK ICE CREAM

Both cultured whole buttermilk and the more widely available low-fat work just fine for this recipe.

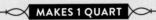

MAKES 1 QUART

1 cup / 237 ml heavy cream

6 large egg yolks

½ cup / 100 g granulated sugar

¼ teaspoon fine salt

1 cup / 237 ml buttermilk

½ teaspoon vanilla extract

1 teaspoon freshly squeezed
lemon juice

In a medium saucepan over medium heat, heat the cream until steaming but not bubbling.

In a medium bowl, whisk the egg yolks and sugar until blended. Gradually whisk the hot cream into the egg yolk mixture until smooth.

Pour the tempered yolk mixture into the saucepan and set over medium-low heat, stirring constantly, until the mixture thickens to a custard (it should coat, rather than run right off of, the back of a wooden spoon or rubber spatula), about 6 minutes. Do not let it boil.

Strain the custard through a fine-mesh sieve into a large bowl and stir in the salt, buttermilk, vanilla, and lemon juice. Transfer the bowl to the refrigerator to chill the custard until cold all the way through, about 2 hours.

Transfer the chilled custard to an ice cream maker and process according to the manufacturer's instructions. Scoop the ice cream into an airtight container and freeze overnight before serving.

GINGER ICE CREAM

With a zing of ginger that suits itself to any season—warming in fall and winter, bright and fresh in spring and summer—this creamy confection partners beautifully with virtually any fruit pie. Note that the custard needs to steep overnight before being processed in an ice cream maker.

◄ **MAKES 1 QUART** ►

5 large egg yolks

1 cup / 237 ml whole milk

½ cup / 100 g granulated sugar

½ teaspoon fine salt

¼ cup / 35 g peeled and julienned fresh ginger

2 cups / 473 ml heavy cream

1 teaspoon vanilla extract

2 tablespoons finely chopped candied ginger

Whisk the egg yolks together in a medium bowl.

Combine the milk, sugar, and salt in a medium saucepan and set over medium heat until steaming but not bubbling. Gradually whisk the hot milk mixture into the egg yolks, pouring in a thin stream and whisking constantly.

Pour the tempered yolk mixture into the saucepan, set over medium-low heat, and stir constantly, until the mixture thickens to a custard (it should coat, rather than run right off, the back of a wooden spoon or rubber spatula), about 6 minutes. Do not let it boil. Take the pan off of the heat, stir in the fresh ginger, cover, cool to room temperature, then transfer to the refrigerator and let steep overnight.

Strain the custard through a fine-mesh sieve into a large bowl and stir in the cream and vanilla. Transfer the bowl to the refrigerator and chill the custard thoroughly, about 2 hours.

Transfer the chilled custard to an ice cream maker and process according to the manufacturer's instructions, stirring in the candied ginger in the last 5 minutes of processing. Scoop the ice cream into an airtight container and freeze overnight before serving.

MAPLE BOURBON ICE CREAM

Maple bourbon has a lovely, toasty-smoky sweetness that pairs beautifully with Coffee-Chocolate-Pecan Pie (page 179), autumnal fruit pies like Apple Cranberry Walnut Lattice (page 51), and aromatic fruit pies such as Five-Spice Plum (page 118). It is widely available these days from various labels, from Jim Beam to Knob Creek.

◄ MAKES 1 QUART ►

1 cup / 237 ml whole milk

3 large egg yolks

¾ cup / 150 g granulated sugar

⅛ teaspoon fine salt

1 cup / 340 g maple syrup,
preferably grade B dark amber

2 cups / 473 ml heavy cream

1 teaspoon maple extract

2 tablespoons maple bourbon

In a medium saucepan over medium heat, heat the milk until steaming but not bubbling.

In a medium bowl, whisk together the egg yolks, sugar, and salt until smooth. Gradually whisk the hot milk into the egg yolk mixture, pouring in a thin stream and whisking constantly.

Pour the tempered yolk mixture into the saucepan, set over medium-low heat, and stir constantly until it thickens to a custard (it should coat, rather than run right off, the back of a wooden spoon or rubber spatula), about 6 minutes. Do not let the custard boil.

Strain the custard through a fine-mesh sieve into a large bowl. Stir in the maple syrup and set the bowl in the refrigerator to chill thoroughly, about 2 hours.

Stir the heavy cream, maple extract, and bourbon into the chilled custard. Transfer the mixture to an ice cream maker and process according to the manufacturer's instructions. Scoop the ice cream into an airtight container and freeze overnight before serving.

ICE CREAM PIE

It is a happy fact of life that there comes a time, every now and then, when there is just more pie than you can manage—like just after you've hosted a big holiday dinner. The perfect solution: Chop up that leftover pie, fold the chunks into a quart of softened ice cream of a compatible flavor, and spread the mixture into the press-in piecrust of your choice (gingersnap, chocolate cookie, or granola). And voilà, *you have a pie within a pie! You can put this one in the freezer for later, when you've recovered from pie overload; your ice cream pie keeps well for up to 2 months. Get creative with the pairings of pie, ice cream, and crust. If the pie has a special topping, top the filled pie with it before freezing (bake the crumb before using it as topping).*

MAKES 1 (9-inch / 23-cm) **PIE**

1 quart ice cream, slightly softened

1½ cups chopped pie, including crust

1 recipe Gingersnap (page 69), Chocolate Cookie (page 156), or Granola (page 167) Crust

Chocolate Cookie Crumb (page 156), Peanut Butter Oatmeal Crumb (page 55), Pretzel Crunch (page 149), Almond Crumb (page 85), or other crumb topping (optional), baked and cooled

Lightly sweetened freshly whipped cream, for serving

Combine the softened ice cream and pie chunks in a medium bowl and use a rubber spatula to gently fold them together. Spread the mixture into the prepared piecrust. Add crumb topping, if using. Cover tightly with plastic wrap and freeze until firm, about 3 hours or up to 2 months.

Let the pie stand at room temperature for about 10 minutes before cutting and serving. Serve with whipped cream.

(mostly) creamy pies

t O ME, FRUIT PIES ARE A CELEBRATION OF THE SEASON IN DESSERT FORM. REVELING IN THE FLAVOR AND TEXTURE OF EACH FRESH FRUIT AT ITS PEAK IS WHAT THOSE PIES ARE ALL ABOUT. BUT THIS CHAPTER IS DEVOTED TO ALL THE OTHER SORTS OF SWEET PIES, WHICH ARE SOMETHING ELSE ALTOGETHER: A CELEBRATION OF DESSERT, PERIOD. THE PIES IN THIS CHAPTER RUN THE GAMUT FROM DENSE CUSTARDS TO AIRY MOUSSES AND FROM SILKY SMOOTH TO CHEWY GOOEY TO CRUNCHY.

One of my missions as a crafter and purveyor of pies is to take the great stalwarts of the American pie tradition—coconut, pecan, sweet potato, banana pudding, great-grandmom's butterscotch, to name just a few here in the non-fruit arena—and bring a little something new to each one, an artisanal touch that makes a deservedly classic confection even better.

So coconut cream pie—without which my family's Christmas would just not be Christmas—becomes richer, yummier, and a whole lot more coconutty with the addition of coconut milk and a wee dram of Jamaican rum (page 145). Pecan pie retains its luscious goo, but the intense syrupiness gets balanced out—and the flavor of the pecans is piqued—by a combination of coffee, chocolate, and cinnamon (page 179). Sweet potatoes are roasted, the better to bring out their rich sweet flavor and silky texture (page 142). Banana pudding pie really is better than ever when you make a sumptuous custard filling from scratch and embed it with little Nilla-wafer-and-banana-slice sandwiches (page 183). And my mom and grandmother assure me that my great grandmom (the family's great pie baker, who inspired all three of us) would approve of my trib-

ute version of her butterscotch pie, with bourbon making the richness even more transcendent (page 160).

And there is a whole world of uncharted territory beyond the classic pies: all the other desserts that—to my mind, as a creator, baker, seller, and proselytizer of pie—merit conversion into pie form. Favorite cookies, candy bars, holiday confections, sandwich spreads, ice cream flavors, beverages, snack foods—it's all fair game. Noteworthy pie creations in that realm include Oatmeal Cookie (page 150), Nutter Butter (page 138), Peppermint Mousse Black Bottom (page 170), Eggnog Cream (page 172), Cookies and Cream (page 155), Chocolate Peanut Butter Mousse with Pretzel Crunch (page 147), and Granola S'more (page 166).

As with fruit pies, a good long chill is essential for most of the pies in this chapter. Most mousse pies are ready after eight hours in the fridge, but custard and cream pies need a good twelve hours to fully firm up. Happily, there are a few exceptions—pies that are ready to slice and serve shortly after they come out of the oven: Breakfast Oatmeal (page 135), Sweet Crumb (page 152), Shoofly (page 176), and Cookie Dough Hand Pies (page 187).

CORNSTARCH CAVEAT

Cornstarch is very useful for thickening pie fillings; it is much more efficient than flour, doesn't impart a bitter flavor, and yields a silkier texture for puddings, custards, and pastry creams.

But here's the thing. It is essential to "cook out" the cornstarch. That's why, in all the creamy pie recipes in this book, you'll see that the custard mixture needs to continue bubbling for at least two minutes after it has thickened to a pudding consistency and reached a boil. If not, the cornstarch may not hit a high enough temperature to fully transform its individual grains, and that can make for a chalky, rather than sumptuously silky, texture.

For fruit pies, the critical point comes during the baking: The reason the filling needs to be bubbling vigorously before you pull your pie out of the oven is because those bubbles tell you that the cornstarch has come to a sustained boil, thus activating the thickening power and helping to ensure that the fruit juices are nicely jelled rather than loose and runny. Remember the other indispensible step for pie filling that holds firm when you slice it: letting it sit—and all those juices set—until the day after you bake it!

⟨ *Whipping Cream* ⟩

▶ Use true heavy cream, which has 36% to 40% milkfat and makes lush, dense, resilient whipped cream. Skip the cartons labeled "whipping cream," which has a lower milkfat content (about 30%).

▶ You can whip by hand (with a large whisk) or with a handheld mixer (either regular beaters or a whisk attachment will work). A stand mixer works well only if you use a whisk attachment *and* put enough cream in the bowl to make plenty of contact with the whisk.

▶ Keep the cream as cold as possible—that means leave it in the fridge until the very moment you're ready to whip it, and if it's a hot day, be sure to work quickly (you can even freeze your bowl and whisk).

▶ If you're using an electric mixer, keep the speed at medium to medium-high rather than cranking it all the way up. High speed makes it too easy to go too far too fast; before you know it you've blown right through all the peak stages and you've got a grainy blob. (This you can salvage by adding a few tablespoons more cream and gradually re-whipping on low speed or by hand with a whisk. But if you can see bits of butterfat, it means you've broken the fat apart and you cannot restore it to creaminess. Your only recourse here would be to beat it a bit more, salt lightly, and use it as butter.)

▶ It only takes a few minutes to whip cream to perfect peaks, but it does keep well for several hours if covered tightly and refrigerated, so you can prep it in advance if need be—just re-whip lightly with a whisk before dolloping onto your pie.

▶ Whipping liquid cream causes its volume to double, so a wee half-pint (4-ounce) carton will give you 2 cups of whipped cream, a pint will become 4 cups, and so on.

▶ Begin whipping and look for the "soft plop": After being whipped for a few minutes, the cream will become a bubbly froth, then "trails" will begin to form after the whisk that don't immediately disappear (fig. 1). That's what's known as the soft plop stage. (Appetizing, I know.) The cream will be just beginning to cling to your whisk or beater if you lift it out of the cream at this stage.

▶ Continue whipping and you get "soft peaks": Lift your whisk out of the bowl and cream will cling to it and form peaks, but these will soften quickly (fig. 2). Keep a very close eye on the cream from this point onward.

▶ Next come "medium-soft peaks": Volume builds, the trails become more distinct, and if you lift up your whisk over the bowl, a peak of cream will form on the end, but the point at the tip will be soft enough to curl adorably to the side (fig. 3). This is the perfect consistency for whipped cream to top a pie.

▶ Keep on whipping and, sooner than you think, you'll have "medium peaks": Do the same test and the peak on the end of the whisk holds its shape. Beware. From here onward, the cream rapidly gets firmer and stiffer, quickly becoming grainy and ultimately going the butter route.

〈 Whipping Egg Whites 〉

Many Magpie pie fillings—from batters to mousses, custards, and creams—get a lofty boost from whipped egg whites. One of the great miracles of culinary science, whipped egg whites are also the foundation for three of our best beloved extras: the Vanilla Meringue (page 63) that makes an ethereal confection out of our Lemon Meringue Pie (see Spin, page 72) and Cranberry Curd Mini Meringue Pies (page 61); the cloud-like Vanilla Marshmallow (page 168) that completes each slice of our Granola S'more Pie (page 166); and the Marshmallow Puff (page 188) that makes our Chocolate Pillow Puff Pie (page 186) oh so dreamy.

Now, I have zero tolerance for undue fussiness, but success with whipping egg whites is one aspect of baking that depends on being pretty clinical: There must be nary a speck of yolk nor a trace of grease, or your whites will flop rather than fluff. So separate your eggs when they are cold and the yolks are less prone to breaking, and have an extra bowl right in front of you as a safety net (so you can pitch in there any eggs whose yolks begin to break, rather than ruin your whole batch of whites).

▶ Use a very clean and very dry metal or glass bowl (steer clear of grease-retaining plastic), beaters/whisk attachment, and rubber spatula. (To guarantee everything's grease-free, you can wipe down your bowl, whisk/beaters, and rubber spatula with distilled white vinegar or lemon juice—then wipe them bone-dry with paper towels.)

▶ Let the egg whites come to room temperature so they will whip to greater volume. (You can bring cold whites to room temperature by putting the bowl in a larger bowl of warm, not hot, water.)

▶ Use a handheld electric mixer or a stand mixer (as long as you have enough whites in the bowl for the whisk attachment to make full contact). You can whip by hand with a whisk, but it takes a long time and lots of elbow grease.

▶ Start with the whites in the bowl, along with any cream of tartar and/or salt called for in the recipe.

▶ Whip gradually, starting at low speed.

▶ Be on the lookout for the egg whites to foam and thicken (fig. 1).

- Beat to soft peaks: a beater lifted out and inverted will have a blob of egg white with a peak that droops over (fig. 2).

- Once soft peaks form, begin to gradually add any sugar called for in the recipe.

- Continue whipping at medium speed until the egg whites form stiff, glossy peaks that hold firm when you invert the beater (fig. 3).

- Stop frequently throughout the process to check your progress and make sure you don't overbeat; this dries out the egg whites, which means they will break down when added to the other ingredients and add weight, rather than airiness, to the end product.

- Use the whites as soon as they reach the stiff peak stage.

- To incorporate whipped egg whites into other ingredients without deflating them, use a rubber spatula to *fold* them in—this means hold the spatula with a flat side facing you, draw it gently downward to slice through the center of the mixture, and then scoop upward, turning the bowl and repeating just until no thick white streaks remain.

breakfast oatmeal pie

Pie for breakfast? Most definitely! This humble pie is easy to make (especially if you have a sheet of dough in the freezer—always a good idea) and mighty delicious. See page 136 for a few fun variations, but also know that you can sub in pretty much any fruit for the blackberries—blueberries, raspberries, or cranberries; a couple of apples that sat in the fridge a little too long; a peach or two that got a little overripe. Note that the oatmeal mixture has to soak in the refrigerator overnight (like a classic Swiss muesli) before it gets combined with the fruit, put into the pie shell, and baked.

MAKES 1 (9-inch / 23-cm) PIE

2 cups / 200 g rolled oats

½ cup / 96 g granulated sugar

1 teaspoon baking powder

1 teaspoon ground cinnamon

½ teaspoon ground ginger

⅛ teaspoon ground or freshly grated nutmeg

½ teaspoon fine salt

2 cups / 473 ml whole milk

1 large egg

3 tablespoons unsalted butter, melted and cooled

2 teaspoons vanilla extract

½ recipe Magpie Dough for Flaky Piecrust (page 17), chilled overnight

1 ripe banana

1 cup blackberries or other fresh fruit

1 tablespoon raw sugar

Maple syrup or honey, for serving

Vanilla yogurt or sweetened whipped cream, for serving

Additional fresh fruit, for serving (optional)

To make the oatmeal filling, whisk the oats, granulated sugar, baking powder, spices, and salt together in a large bowl.

In a small bowl, whisk together the milk, egg, butter, and vanilla. Add the milk mixture to the oatmeal mixture and stir to combine. Cover with plastic wrap and chill overnight.

Roll, pan, and flute the dough as directed on pages 20–23, then follow the instructions on page 24 to fully prebake the crust. Set the pan on a wire rack and let the shell cool while you make the filling.

(Continued)

To assemble and bake the pie, preheat the oven to 350°F (175°C) with a rack in the center. Line a baking sheet with parchment paper.

Cut the banana into ¼-inch-thick slices and layer evenly across the bottom of the prepared pie shell. Spoon half of the oatmeal mixture over the banana and spread evenly, then layer on the blackberries. Top with the remaining oatmeal mixture, spreading evenly. Sprinkle the raw sugar all over the top of the pie.

Bake the pie on the parchment-lined baking sheet for 35 to 45 minutes, or until the filling is puffed in the center and lightly browned around the edges, rotating halfway through the baking time.

Transfer the pan to a wire rack and cool the pie 10 minutes before slicing and serving, warm, with your choice of the toppings.

Tropical Oatmeal Pie: Replace the blackberries with diced mango and add ½ cup (40 g) toasted coconut to the oatmeal mixture; serve with agave syrup.

Savory Apple Oatmeal Pie: Replace the blackberries with diced apples mixed with 2 strips bacon, cooked and crumbled; serve with maple syrup.

Trail Mix Oatmeal Pie: Omit the blackberries and add ½ cup (170 g) mixed dried fruit to the oatmeal mixture; serve with honey and yogurt.

peanut butter and jam pie

Light, creamy peanut butter mousse blankets a layer of jam in a pie that's as easy to make as it is to love. If you are going to keep the pie for a few days (or use fruit spread, which typically lacks the natural pectin thickener found in jam), it's a good idea to include the optional gelatin—that's what we do in the shop to ensure the pie sets up nicely and holds firm when sliced.

MAKES 1 (9-inch / 23-cm) PIE

½ recipe Magpie Dough for Flaky Piecrust (page 17), chilled overnight

1 (10-ounce) jar strawberry, grape, or raspberry jam

2½ teaspoons powdered unflavored gelatin (optional)

8 ounces / 226 g cream cheese

1 cup / 256 g creamy peanut butter

½ cup plus 1 tablespoon / 115 g granulated sugar

½ teaspoon vanilla extract

Pinch fine salt

1¼ cups / 312 ml cold heavy cream

Lightly sweetened freshly whipped cream, for serving

Roll, pan, and flute the dough as directed on pages 20–23, then follow the directions on page 24 to fully prebake the piecrust. Set the pan on a wire rack and let the shell cool completely to room temperature while you make the filling.

In a medium saucepan, melt the jam over medium heat until it is smooth and loose, stirring constantly, 3 to 4 minutes. Take the pan off the heat. (If you want to use the gelatin, first soften it in 1 tablespoon of cold water for 5 minutes, then whisk it into the melted jam and stir well to blend, making sure it's not grainy.)

Spread the warm jam evenly across the bottom of the pie shell and set in the refrigerator to chill while you prepare the peanut butter filling.

(Continued)

In the bowl of a stand mixer fitted with the paddle attachment, combine the cream cheese, peanut butter, sugar, vanilla, and salt and beat at medium speed until smooth, stopping occasionally to scrape down the sides of the bowl, 5 to 7 minutes.

In a separate bowl, whip the cream to medium peaks (see Whipping Cream, page 130).

Gently fold a third of the whipped cream into the peanut butter mixture until uniformly combined. Fold in the remaining whipped cream until no white streaks remain.

Scoop the peanut butter mousse into the jam-lined pie shell, spreading evenly and smoothing the top. Cover the pie with plastic wrap and chill overnight (at least 12 hours and up to 3 days) before slicing and serving, cold, with the sweetened whipped cream.

Nutter Butter Pie: Omit the jam and prepare the pie as directed. Cover the pie with plastic wrap and refrigerate overnight. Follow the instructions on page 149 for slicing the pie before topping with Peanut Butter Oatmeal Crumb (page 55); serve cold with sweetened whipped cream.

café mocha pie

Chocolate-bottom pies are easy to make and look impressive. It's as easy as pouring some hot custard onto chopped chocolate, whisking to melt and blend together, and spreading on the bottom of the pie shell. In the following recipe, coffee goes in the mix to give the chocolate layer a mocha tinge, and it's topped off with a café mousse. You could use the same method to sneak a chocolate layer into all sorts of cream and pudding pies.

◄ MAKES 1 (9-inch / 23-cm) PIE ►

½ recipe Magpie Dough for Flaky Piecrust (page 17), chilled overnight

4 ounces / 120 g semisweet chocolate

2 tablespoons instant coffee

2½ cups / 591 ml whole milk, divided

¾ cup / 150 g granulated sugar

¼ cup / 35 g cornstarch

¼ teaspoon fine salt

4 large egg yolks

2 tablespoons unsalted butter

½ teaspoon vanilla extract

1¼ teaspoons unflavored powdered gelatin

1 cup / 237 ml heavy cream

Lightly sweetened freshly whipped cream, for serving

Shaved chocolate, for serving

Roll, pan, and flute the dough as directed on pages 20–23, then follow the directions on page 24 to fully prebake the crust. Set the pan on a wire rack to cool while you make the filling.

To make the mocha custard, chop the chocolate and set it aside in a medium bowl.

Combine the instant coffee and 2¼ cups of the milk in a medium sauce-pan and set over medium heat, stirring occasionally, until the mixture is steaming (do not boil!). Keep warm over very low heat.

Whisk the sugar, cornstarch, and salt together in a mixing bowl. Whisk in the egg yolks until the mixture is smooth and pale. Immediately measure out 1 cup of the hot milk mixture and slowly whisk it into the yolk mixture, pouring in a thin stream and whisking constantly until combined.

Turn the heat under the saucepan back up to medium and slowly add the tempered yolks, pouring in a thin stream and whisking constantly. Continue cooking, whisking constantly, until the mixture thickens to a pudding consistency and a few large bubbles rise to the surface, about 5 minutes. Once the bubbles appear, continue cooking the custard, whisk-ing constantly, for 2 more minutes.

(Continued)

Remove the pan from the heat and whisk in the butter and vanilla.

Measure out 1 cup of the hot custard, add it to the chopped chocolate and let stand 2 minutes, then whisk until smooth and creamy. Scoop the mocha custard into the prepared pie shell, spreading evenly. Transfer the pie to the refrigerator to chill and set the mocha custard (10 to 15 minutes) while you make the café mousse.

To make the café mousse, sprinkle the gelatin onto the surface of the remaining ¼ cup milk and let soften for 5 minutes.

Transfer the remaining custard from the saucepan to a medium bowl and whisk in the bloomed gelatin. Refrigerate until cool, 15 to 20 minutes, whisking at 5-minute intervals to prevent the edges from setting.

Whip the cream to medium peaks (see Whipping Cream, page 130).

Whisk one-third of the whipped cream into the cooled custard, then gently fold in the remaining whipped cream, just until faint white streaks remain.

Retrieve the pie from the refrigerator. Spread the mousse evenly over the mocha custard layer, smoothing the top. Cover the pie with plastic wrap, return it to the refrigerator, and chill overnight (at least 8 hours and up to 3 days) before slicing and serving, cold, with whipped cream and chocolate shavings.

spin

Nightcap Mocha Pie: *Whisk 1 tablespoon of your favorite coffee-friendly spirits—crème de menthe, amaretto, or hazelnut liqueur—into the custard along with the bloomed gelatin.*

roasted sweet potato pie

Steer clear of pale whitish-yellow sweet potatoes for this pie; their starchy, crumbly flesh wouldn't give you the silky and sumptuous, bright orange filling that makes this pie a big favorite at Magpie. Ever had sweet potato pie that had a distinctly vegetal taste and heavy, wet texture? Chances are the filling was made with steamed, boiled, or even frozen-then-nuked sweet potatoes. Roasting the sweet potatoes, rather than boiling or steaming them, concentrates their natural sugars and gives the flesh a rich, caramelly flavor.

◆ MAKES 1 (9-inch / 23-cm) PIE ◆

½ recipe Magpie Dough for Flaky Piecrust (page 17), chilled overnight

2 medium-sized orange-flesh sweet potatoes

1 tablespoon freshly squeezed lemon juice

½ cup / 100 g granulated sugar

½ cup / 110 g packed light brown sugar

3 tablespoons unsalted butter, melted and cooled

¼ teaspoon ground or freshly grated nutmeg

¾ teaspoon ground cinnamon

¾ teaspoon fine salt

¾ cup / 177 ml heavy cream

2 large eggs

½ teaspoon freshly grated orange zest

2 teaspoons vanilla extract

2 teaspoons Jamaican rum (we use Appleton Estate Special Gold at the shop)

Lightly sweetened freshly whipped cream, for serving

Ginger Ice Cream (page 123), for serving

Roll, pan, and flute the dough as directed on page 20–23, then follow the directions on page 24 to parbake the crust. Set the pan on a wire rack and let the shell cool while you make the filling.

To bake the sweet potatoes, preheat the oven to 400°F (200°C) with a rack in the center. Line a rimmed baking sheet with parchment paper.

Use a fork to pierce each sweet potato several times. Set them on the prepared baking sheet and bake until tender (when a small knife inserted deep into the potato comes out easily), about 45 minutes.

Set the roasted sweet potatoes aside until cool enough to handle, then cut them in half lengthwise and scoop the flesh out of the skins and into the bowl of a food processor. (Set the baking sheet aside for baking the pie.) Add the lemon juice and purée until the mixture is very smooth, about 30 seconds.

To make the filling and bake the pie, preheat the oven to 350°F (175°C).

Combine the sugars, butter, nutmeg, cinnamon, and salt in a large mixing bowl and use a handheld electric mixer fitted with a whisk attachment to whip the ingredients together at medium speed. Add the cream, eggs, orange zest, vanilla, and rum and beat together at medium speed until combined. Add the purée and continue mixing at medium speed until smooth and uniform.

Scoop the filling into the parbaked pie shell, spreading evenly and smoothing the top.

Set the pan on the same baking sheet you used for the sweet potatoes (change the parchment if you'd like) and bake the pie 30 minutes, rotating halfway through the baking time. The pie is done when the filling is puffed and set around the edges but still has a slight jiggle to it in the center.

Transfer the pan to a wire rack and cool the pie completely to room temperature, then cover loosely with plastic wrap and chill overnight (at least 12 hours or up to 3 days) before slicing and serving with sweetened whipped cream and ginger ice cream.

Sweet Potato Meringue Pie:
Top each slice of chilled pie with a vanilla marshmallow (page 168), use a kitchen torch to lightly toast the marshmallow, and serve immediately.

coconut rum pie

Coconut milk gives this pie full, lush coconut flavor. Toasted coconut chips make a really nice accompaniment; they're sold in small bags at most health food stores.

MAKES 1 (9-inch / 23-cm) PIE

½ recipe Magpie Dough for Flaky Piecrust (page 17), chilled overnight

½ cup / 57 g sweetened coconut flakes

¾ cup / 150 g granulated sugar, divided

1 (14-ounce / 403-ml) can coconut milk

1 cup / 237 ml whole milk

¼ teaspoon fine salt

¼ cup / 30 g cornstarch

5 large egg yolks

2 tablespoons unsalted butter, cut in pieces, at room temperature

1½ teaspoons vanilla extract

2 teaspoons Jamaican rum (we use Appleton Estate Special Gold at the shop)

1 teaspoon coconut extract

Lightly sweetened freshly whipped cream, for serving

½ cup / 40 g toasted coconut chips, for serving

Roll, pan, and flute the dough as directed on pages 20–23, then follow the instructions on page 24 to fully prebake the piecrust. Set the pan on a wire rack and let the shell cool to room temperature while you make the filling.

Combine the coconut flakes and half of the sugar (6 tablespoons) in the bowl of a food processor and pulse the machine until the flakes are finely minced.

Combine the flake coconut mixture with the coconut milk and whole milk in a medium saucepan and heat over medium heat, stirring occasionally, until steaming (don't boil!). Keep warm over very low heat.

(Continued)

Combine the remaining 6 tablespoons sugar with salt and cornstarch in a bowl, whisking to mix. Add the egg yolks and whisk until smooth and pale. Immediately measure out 1 cup of the hot milk mixture and slowly add it to the egg yolk mixture, pouring in a thin stream and whisking constantly until combined.

Slowly add the tempered yolks to the saucepan, pouring in a thin stream and whisking constantly. Turn the heat under the pan back up to medium. Cook, whisking constantly, until the mixture thickens to a pudding consistency and a few large bubbles rise to the surface, about 5 minutes. Once the bubbles appear, cook the custard 2 more minutes, whisking constantly.

Remove the pan from the heat and whisk in the butter, vanilla, rum, and coconut extract until smooth. Let cool 5 minutes.

Scoop the filling into the prepared pie shell, spreading evenly and smoothing the top. Cover with plastic wrap, pressing onto the surface of the pudding and chill overnight (at least 12 hours and up to 3 days) before slicing and serving.

Serve cold, each slice topped with a dollop of whipped cream and toasted coconut chips.

spins

Coconut Granola Pie: *Replace the flaky piecrust with Granola Crust (page 167).*

Coconut Chocolate Cookie Pie: *Instead of flaky piecrust, go with Chocolate Cookie Crust (page 156).*

chocolate peanut butter mousse pie with pretzel crunch

It is no accident that this pie is reminiscent of the chocolate peanut butter–covered pretzels you can get at Chocolate by Mueller in Philadelphia's Reading Terminal Market. Those are one of my favorite sweet treats; the sweet-salty crunch is perfectly balanced and just plain scrumptious.

MAKES 1 (9-inch / 23-cm) PIE

½ recipe Magpie Dough for Flaky Piecrust (page 17), chilled overnight

1 (4-ounce / 113 g) bar semisweet chocolate

⅓ cup plus 2 tablespoons / 91 g granulated sugar

⅔ cup / 158 ml whole milk, divided

¾ cup / 195 g creamy peanut butter

¼ teaspoon kosher salt

1 teaspoon unflavored powdered gelatin

1½ cups / 355 ml heavy cream

Pretzel Crunch (page 149), for topping

Lightly sweetened freshly whipped cream, for serving (optional)

Roll, pan, and flute the dough as directed on page 20–23, then follow the instructions on page 24 to fully prebake the piecrust. Set the pan on a wire rack and let the shell cool to room temperature while you make the filling.

To make the filling, coarsely chop the chocolate and set it aside in a large bowl.

Combine the sugar and 7 tablespoons of the milk in a medium saucepan and heat over medium heat, stirring occasionally, until steaming (do not boil). Whisk in the peanut butter until smooth.

Take the pan off the heat and pour the hot milk mixture over the chocolate, whisking until the chocolate is melted and the mixture is smooth. Whisk in the salt.

Pour the remaining milk (you'll have about 3 to 4 tablespoons) into a small microwavable bowl. Sprinkle the gelatin onto the surface of the milk and let stand 5 minutes, then microwave at half power for 10 seconds to ensure that the gelatin is dissolved (the mixture should feel smooth between your fingertips).

(Continued)

147

Whisk the bloomed gelatin into the warm chocolate peanut butter mixture. Set aside to cool to room temperature, stirring occasionally to help cool the mixture evenly and prevent it from setting around the edges. (Don't leave it sitting after it's cooled or it will stiffen.)

Whip the cream to medium peaks (see Whipping Cream, page 130). Gently fold the whipped cream into the chocolate mixture in thirds, mixing the last third just until no white streaks remain. Scoop the mousse into the prepared crust, smoothing the top. Cover with plastic wrap and chill overnight (at least 8 hours or up to 3 days) before slicing and serving.

To serve the pie, cut into 8 equal slices, leaving the slices in the pan, then top the entire pie with pretzel crunch, pressing the topping lightly into the mousse. Use a pie server to slide each slice onto a serving plate. Garnish with a dollop of whipped cream, if desired.

pretzel crunch

Try not to eat all the crunch before you get any on top of the pie. It's that good.

◄ **MAKES 2 CUPS** ►

4 ounces / 113 g thin pretzel sticks

⅓ cup / 60 g packed light brown sugar

½ teaspoon kosher salt

7 tablespoons / 100 g unsalted butter, melted

Chocolate Peanut Butter Mousse Pie with Chocolate Peanut Crunch:
Instead of the pretzel crunch, top the pie with ¾ cup Chocolate Cookie Crumb (page 156) and 2 to 3 tablespoons chopped cocktail peanuts.

Preheat the oven to 325°F (160°C) with a rack in the center. Line a baking sheet with parchment paper.

In a medium bowl, toss together the pretzels, sugar, and salt. Add the melted butter and toss until evenly coated.

Spread the pretzels on the prepared baking sheet and bake 20 minutes, stirring halfway through.

Leave the pretzel crunch on the tray to cool completely to room temperature. Once cooled, break apart any large clusters.

Store in an airtight container for up to 2 weeks.

oatmeal cookie pie

Inspired by the gooey center of the ideal oatmeal cookie, this pie is easy to make, with a one-bowl filling that goes straight into an un-prebaked crust. It's a major crowd pleaser, especially when served with a scoop of homemade maple bourbon ice cream, any good vanilla ice cream—or a tall glass of cold milk or steaming cup of hot cocoa.

MAKES 1 (9-inch / 23-cm) PIE

½ recipe Magpie Dough for Flaky Piecrust (page 17), chilled overnight

1 cup / 237 ml corn syrup

½ cup plus 1 tablespoon /115 g packed dark brown sugar

½ cup / 96 g granulated sugar

½ cup /113 g unsalted butter, melted and cooled

3 large eggs

1 teaspoon ground cinnamon

¼ teaspoon ground or freshly grated nutmeg

½ teaspoon Chinese five-spice powder

¾ teaspoon fine salt

1¼ cups / 100 g quick-cooking oats

2 tablespoons all-purpose flour

1 teaspoon freshly squeezed lemon juice

1 teaspoon vanilla extract

Maple Bourbon Ice Cream (page 124), for serving (optional)

Roll, pan, and flute the dough as directed on pages 20–23. Set the pan in the refrigerator to chill the shell while you make the filling.

Preheat the oven to 375°F (190°C) with a rack in the center. Line a baking sheet with parchment paper.

Combine the corn syrup and sugars in the bowl of a stand mixer fitted with the whisk attachment and mix on medium-high speed until smooth. Beat in the melted butter, then add the eggs one at a time and mix on medium-high for about 3 minutes, or until the mixture is smooth and foamy. Add the spices, salt, oats, flour, lemon juice, and vanilla and mix on medium speed for 1 minute; the mixture will be smooth and uniformly combined.

Rap the bowl against the counter a couple of times to pop any air bubbles that might have formed below the surface. (These can rise and burst during baking and cause pockmarking across the top of the filling.)

Retrieve the prepared pie shell from the refrigerator and set the pan on the parchment-lined baking sheet. Scoop the filling into the shell, spreading evenly.

Transfer the baking sheet to the oven and bake the pie for 15 minutes. Then rotate the pie, lower the oven temperature to 325°F (160°C), and bake another 22 to 25 minutes, or until the filling has puffed in the center and around the edges, is beautifully browned, and no longer jiggles when tapped.

Transfer the pan to a wire rack and cool the pie to room temperature, then chill overnight (at least 12 hours or up to 3 days) before slicing and serving with maple bourbon ice cream.

sweet crumb pie

Pies with a cake-like element are traditional classics of Pennsylvania German baking: shoofly, Montgomery, and lemon sponge pies all have a cake layer to them. But in sweet crumb pie the entire filling is cakey. Whipped egg whites are the key to its airy loveliness. This pie is especially fun to serve up, as its cakey-pie goodness surprises and delights just about everyone.

◆— MAKES 1 (9-inch / 23-cm) PIE —◆

½ recipe Magpie Dough for Flaky Piecrust (page 17), chilled overnight

1½ cups / 187 g all-purpose flour

1½ teaspoons baking powder

1¼ cups / 235 g packed light brown sugar

½ teaspoon fine salt

½ teaspoon ground cinnamon

4 tablespoons / 56 g unsalted butter, cut in small pieces, at room temperature

2 large eggs, separated

⅔ cup / 158 ml whole milk

1 teaspoon vanilla extract

Lightly sweetened freshly whipped cream, for serving

Fresh berries, for serving

Roll, pan, and flute the dough as directed on page 20–23. Set the pan in the refrigerator to chill the shell while you make the filling.

Preheat the oven to 375°F (190°C) with a rack in the center. Line a baking sheet with parchment paper.

Whisk the flour, baking powder, brown sugar, salt, and cinnamon together in a large bowl. Add the butter and mix with your hands until crumbly. Measure out and reserve ¼ cup of the crumb mixture for the topping.

In a medium bowl, whisk together the egg yolks, milk, and vanilla. Add the milk mixture to the crumb mixture remaining in the large bowl, whisking until a smooth batter forms.

In a separate clean, dry bowl, whip the egg whites to stiff peaks (see Whipping Egg Whites, page 130). Gently fold the egg whites into the batter just until no white streaks remain.

Set the prepared pie shell on the parchment-lined baking sheet. Pour the batter into the pie shell and smooth the top. Sprinkle evenly with the reserved crumb.

Bake the pie 30 to 40 minutes, or until a tester inserted in the center comes out with just a few crumbs attached, rotating halfway through the baking time.

Set the pan on a wire rack and let the pie cool completely to room temperature before slicing and serving, topped with whipped cream and fresh berries.

Berry Sweet Crumb Pie:
Mix a few handfuls of the berries of your choice into the batter just before folding in the egg whites.

cookies and cream pie

White chocolate gives this pie the rich, silky sweetness of cookies and cream ice cream.

◄ MAKES 1 (9-inch / 23-cm) PIE ►

6 ounces /165 g white chocolate

1 recipe Chocolate Cookie Crumb (page 156), divided

1 recipe Chocolate Cookie Crust (page 156)

½ cup plus 2 tablespoons / 148 ml whole milk

2 teaspoons unflavored powdered gelatin

¼ teaspoon fine salt

2 cups / 473 ml heavy cream

Lightly sweetened freshly whipped cream, for serving

Chop the white chocolate, put it in a large bowl, and set aside. Make the cookie crumb and cookie crust as directed on page 156 and let cool while you make the fillings.

Pour the milk into a medium saucepan and sprinkle the gelatin across the surface. Let it sit 5 minutes, then stir the softened gelatin into the milk and warm the mixture over medium-low heat until the gelatin has dissolved, about 1 minute.

Remove the pan from the heat. Pour the hot milk over the white chocolate, let sit 5 minutes, then whisk until smooth. Whisk in the salt and let the mixture cool to room temperature, whisking from time to time (the consistency will become thick and syrupy, resembling sweetened condensed milk).

Whip the cream to medium peaks (see Whipping Cream, page 130). Fold a third of the whipped cream into the white chocolate mixture until smooth. Gently fold in the remaining whipped cream until no white streaks remain.

Fold 1 cup of the chocolate cookie crumb into the white chocolate mousse. (Reserve the remaining 1 cup crumb in an airtight container at room temperature until you are ready to slice and serve the pie.)

Scoop the mousse into the prepared crust, spreading evenly. Chill overnight (at least 8 hours and up to 3 days) before slicing and serving.

(Continued)

To serve the pie, cut 8 equal slices, leaving the slices in the pan, then top the entire pie with ½ cup of the remaining cookie crumb, pressing the topping lightly into the mousse. Use a pie server to slide each slice onto a serving plate. Garnish with a dollop of sweetened whipped cream and reserved cookie crumbs.

chocolate cookie crumb or crust

For the Cookies and Cream Pie (page 155), double this recipe to make 1 piecrust and 2 cups crumb topping.

MAKES 2 CUPS CRUMB TOPPING OR 1 (9-inch / 23-cm) PIECRUST

⅔ cup / 134 g granulated sugar

⅓ cup plus 1 tablespoon / 50 g all-purpose flour

¼ cup / 28 g good-quality Dutch-process cocoa powder

¼ teaspoon fine salt

4 tablespoons / 56 g unsalted butter, melted and cooled

Preheat the oven to 325°F (160°C) with a rack in the center.

Whisk together the sugar, flour, cocoa, and salt in a medium bowl. Add the melted butter and mix until the mixture is thoroughly combined and you can make a clump by squeezing a bit with your hand.

To make crumb topping: Press the dough into an even layer on a 13 x 9-inch (33 x 23-cm) baking sheet. Bake until set, 8 to 10 minutes. Take the sheet out of the oven and set the pan on a wire rack until cool enough to handle. Break the crumb into ½-inch pieces, then bake until firm, about 6 to 8 additional minutes. Cool completely to room temperature. Store in an airtight container for up to 1 week, or freeze for up to 1 month.

To make a piecrust: Press the dough evenly into a 9-inch (23-cm) pie pan and bake until the sides are set, 8 to 10 minutes. Cool completely before filling or covering with plastic wrap to store 1 day at room temperature. Double wrap to freeze for up to 2 weeks.

nutella florentine pie

The pretty, translucent florentine (wafer cookie) is nice to nibble on between decadently rich bites of this pie, which is filled with something resembling hazelnut fudge.

MAKES 1 (9-inch / 23-cm) PIE

½ recipe Magpie Dough for Flaky Piecrust (page 17), chilled overnight

2 cups / 270 g Nutella

12 ounces / 340 g cold mascarpone cheese

¼ teaspoon fine salt

1 cup / 237 ml heavy cream

Lightly sweetened freshly whipped cream, for serving

8 Hazelnut Florentines (page 158), for serving

Roll, pan, and flute the dough as directed on pages 20–23, then follow the instructions on page 24 to fully prebake the crust. Transfer the pan to a wire rack and let the crust cool while you make the filling.

Combine the Nutella, mascarpone, and salt in a large bowl and use an electric mixer on medium-low speed to beat together until smooth and shiny, 3 to 5 minutes.

Whip the cream to medium peaks (see Whipping Cream, page 130).

Fold the whipped cream into the Nutella mixture until no white streaks remain.

Scoop the mousse into the prepared pie shell and smooth the top. Cover with plastic wrap and refrigerate overnight (at least 8 hours or up to 3 days) before slicing and serving.

Serve cold, topping each slice with whipped cream and a hazelnut florentine.

hazelnut florentine

The dough spreads a lot while baking, so make sure to keep the spacing good and wide when you're spooning it onto the baking sheet. Leftover wafers make a nice little sweet with coffee or tea; or you can break them into shards (and consider dipping them in melted bittersweet chocolate) for a delish ice cream topping.

MAKES ABOUT 12 (2-inch / 5-cm) WAFERS

¼ cup / 23 g hazelnuts

3 tablespoons all-purpose flour

⅛ teaspoon ground cinnamon

⅛ teaspoon fine salt

4 tablespoons / 56 g unsalted butter

5 tablespoons / 60 g granulated sugar

1 tablespoon heavy cream

1½ teaspoons light corn syrup

⅛ teaspoon vanilla extract

⅛ teaspoon hazelnut extract (optional)

Preheat the oven to 350°F (175°C) with a rack in the center. Line 2 baking sheets with parchment paper.

Toast the hazelnuts on one of the prepared baking sheets for 5 minutes, or just until lightly brown and aromatic. Let the nuts cool, then transfer them to a clean dishtowel and rub to remove the skins.

Line the baking sheet with fresh parchment paper.

In the bowl of a food processor, combine the nuts, flour, cinnamon, and salt and pulse until the nuts are pulverized, about 1 minute. Transfer the mixture to a large bowl.

Combine the butter, sugar, heavy cream, and syrup in a medium saucepan and stir to mix. Bring the mixture to a boil over high heat. Boil the mixture without stirring for 1 full minute, at which point it will be a light gold color, then remove the pan from the heat and stir in the vanilla and hazelnut extract (if using).

Pour the caramel over the nut mixture and stir to combine. Set aside to cool to room temperature, at least 30 minutes. The mixture will firm up to a soft caramel consistency. (At this point the dough can be transferred to an air-tight container and refrigerated overnight before scooping and baking.)

Use a ½-teaspoon measure to scoop the dough into small balls and place them 3 inches apart on the prepared baking sheets. Bake until the cookies are thin and golden brown, 7 to 9 minutes. The cookies will be soft.

Let the cookies cool on the baking sheets for about 5 minutes to allow them to set up a little. Line 2 wire racks with paper towels, then use a thin metal spatula to carefully transfer the cookies to the paper towels. Let them sit a few minutes to allow the paper towels to absorb excess oil, then carefully flip the cookies and let sit a few more minutes.

Store in an airtight container at room temperature up to 3 days.

butterscotch bourbon pie

This pie, Magpie's specialty of the house, has been with us since Day One. It's based on a recipe from my maternal great-grandmother, Florence June Dunkelberger Willhide; her handwritten recipe is framed on the wall near the front door of the shop. Her version was straight butterscotch; mine has bourbon, which deepens the butterscotch flavor. It's important to follow the instructions closely to get the filling to bake up just right—thick, rich custard below, thin sponge cake up top.

❯❮ MAKES 1 (9-inch / 23-cm) PIE ❯❮

½ recipe Magpie Dough for Flaky Piecrust (page 17), chilled overnight

2 tablespoons unsalted butter, at room temperature

1½ cups / 288 g packed dark brown sugar

3 large eggs, separated, at room temperature

2 tablespoons all-purpose flour

½ teaspoon fine salt

1 tablespoon bourbon

1 tablespoon vanilla extract

1½ teaspoons freshly squeezed lemon juice

1 (12-ounce) can evaporated milk

Lightly sweetened freshly whipped cream, for serving

Roll, pan, and flute the dough as directed on pages 20–23. Transfer the pan to the refrigerator and chill the shell while you prepare the filling.

Preheat the oven to 350°F (175°C) with a rack in the center. Line a baking sheet with parchment paper.

Combine the butter, brown sugar, and egg yolks in the bowl of a stand mixer fitted with the paddle attachment. Run the machine on low speed for several minutes to cream the mixture together until it is very light and creamy, pausing occasionally to scrape down the bowl.

Add the flour and salt and mix until no streaks of white are visible, 1 to 2 minutes. The mixture will be heavy and thick, like wet sand.

Add the bourbon, vanilla, and lemon juice and continue mixing on low until well combined, about 2 minutes, at which point it will be even heavier and thicker, like really wet sand.

With the mixer running at low speed, add the evaporated milk and mix until smooth and liquidy, stopping often to scrape down the sides, about 2 minutes.

(Continued)

In a separate clean, dry bowl, whip the egg whites to medium-soft peaks (see Whipping Egg Whites, page 130).

Gently fold one-third of the egg whites into the filling (which will now become clumpy), using a whisk to lift the whites up and over from the bottom of the bowl to incorporate without deflating. Use a rubber spatula to slowly and gently fold in the remaining two-thirds of the egg whites, incorporating just to the point that no white clumps or very white streaks remain. Don't over-mix; the mixture should be a pale cappuccino color, not uniform from top to bottom (foamier on the top).

Retrieve the prepared pie shell from the refrigerator and set the pan on the parchment-lined baking sheet. Pour the filling into the pie shell. Carefully (the filling is very sloshy; try to keep the tray steady) transfer the baking sheet to the oven and bake the pie 45 minutes, or until the top is deeply browned and puffed and the center is still ever-so-slightly loose (it should give a bit of a wiggle when you tap the edge of the baking sheet).

Carefully transfer the tray from the oven to a wire rack. Let cool completely to room temperature (it sinks as it cools, going from puffed-up and pillowy at the edges to level with the rim of the pan; at the center it will crinkle as it cools and sets), then chill overnight (at least 12 hours and up to 3 days) before slicing and serving. Serve with whipped cream.

chocolate blackout pie

This is a chocolate knockout. Deep dark chocolate pudding pie topped with deep dark chocolate cake crumbs. Lights out. End of story.

MAKES 1 (9-inch / 23-cm) PIE

½ recipe Magpie Dough for Flaky Piecrust (page 17), chilled overnight

2½ cups / 591 ml whole milk

6 tablespoons / 40 g Valrhona cocoa powder

2 teaspoons instant coffee or espresso powder

¾ cup / 150 g granulated sugar

¼ cup / 30 g cornstarch

½ teaspoon fine salt

4 large egg yolks

2 tablespoons unsalted butter, cubed

1 teaspoon vanilla extract

1¼ cups crumbled Chocolate Cake (page 165)

Lightly sweetened freshly whipped cream, for serving

Roll, pan, and flute the dough as directed on pages 20–23, then follow the instructions on page 24 to fully prebake the crust. Set the pan on a wire rack and let the shell cool to room temperature while you make the filling.

Whisk the milk, cocoa, and powdered coffee together in a medium saucepan. Bring the mixture to a simmer over medium heat, stirring occasionally. Keep warm over very low heat.

Whisk the sugar, cornstarch, and salt together in a bowl. Add the yolks and whisk until smooth and pale. Immediately measure out 1 cup of the hot milk mixture and slowly add it to the yolk mixture, pouring in a thin stream and whisking constantly.

Turn the heat under the saucepan back up to medium. Slowly add the tempered yolks into the pan, pouring in a thin stream and whisking constantly. Cook, whisking constantly, until the mixture thickens to a pudding consistency and a few large bubbles rise to the surface, about 5 minutes.

Remove the pan from the heat and whisk in the butter and vanilla extract. Let cool until slightly warm, about 5 minutes, stirring often. (Don't cool it all the way or it will begin to set—if this happens, gently rewarm to remedy.)

Scoop the filling into the prepared pie shell, spreading evenly and smoothing the top. Top with the crumbled cake, pressing gently into the surface of the filling. Cover with plastic wrap and chill overnight (at least 12 hours and up to 3 days) before slicing and serving. Serve with whipped cream.

chocolate cake

You will have at least twice as much cake as needed to top the Chocolate Blackout Pie (page 163). Put the leftover cake in an airtight container or cover it tightly in a double layer of plastic wrap and chuck it in the freezer. You can thaw at room temperature any time over the next couple of months to enjoy as a topping for pretty much any other creamy pie in this book. Or serve it on its own, adding some fresh berries, a little whipped cream, or a scoop of ice cream. It is damn fine cake any which way.

MAKES 1 (8-inch / 20-cm) SQUARE CAKE

¼ cup / 56 g unsalted butter, plus additional for greasing baking dish

¾ cup / 94 g all-purpose flour, plus additional for flouring baking dish

1 teaspoon baking powder

¼ teaspoon baking soda

¼ teaspoon fine salt

6 tablespoons / 40 g high-quality Dutch-process cocoa powder

½ cup / 118 ml brewed coffee

½ cup /118 ml whole milk

½ cup / 55 g packed light brown sugar

½ cup / 100 g granulated sugar

1 large egg

½ teaspoon vanilla extract

Preheat the oven to 325°F (160°C) with a rack in the center. Butter and flour an 8 x 8-inch (20 x 20-cm) baking dish.

Whisk together the flour, baking powder, baking soda, and salt in a bowl.

Melt the butter in a large saucepan over medium heat. Stir in the cocoa and cook until fragrant, about 1 minute. Take the pan off the heat and whisk in the coffee, milk, and sugars, mixing until dissolved and combined. Whisk in the egg and vanilla, then slowly whisk in the flour mixture.

Pour the batter into the prepared pan and bake until a tester inserted in the center of the cake comes out clean, 30 to 35 minutes. Cool the cake in the pan for 15 minutes, then invert onto a wire rack and cool to room temperature.

The cake can be wrapped in plastic wrap, placed in a freezer bag, and frozen up to 1 month.

granola s'more pie

Complete with gooey, slightly scorched marshmallow, this is a real crowd-pleaser—a campfire party in a pie shell. Every summer at the shop, this is our August pie of the month. We top each slice with a big fat 2-inch-square block of homemade marshmallow that's nice and toasty and not too burnt. We came up with a toasting method that allowed us to serve slice after slice after slice with a perfectly melty marshmallow: nuke the marshmallow just until it starts to get oozy, scrape it off the plate and onto a slice of pie, then hit it with the kitchen torch for just a moment. You could also just toast your marshmallow on a skewer over a grill or the flame of a gas stove. Note that the marshmallows need a day's head start before you make the pie (page 168).

MAKES 1 (9-inch / 23-cm) PIE

1 recipe Granola Crust (page 167)

1¼ cups / 312 ml whole milk

3 tablespoons high-quality Dutch process cocoa

4 teaspoons instant coffee or espresso powder

6 tablespoons / 75 g granulated sugar

2 tablespoons cornstarch

⅛ teaspoon fine salt

2 large egg yolks

1 tablespoon unsalted butter, cut into small cubes

1 teaspoon vanilla extract

8 Vanilla Marshmallows (page 168)

Prepare the granola crust as directed on page 167. Set the baked crust on a wire rack and let it cool to room temperature while you make the filling.

Whisk the milk, cocoa, and coffee powder together in a medium saucepan. Cook over medium heat until steaming (don't boil!), stirring occasionally. Keep warm over very low heat.

Whisk the sugar, cornstarch, and salt together in a bowl. Add the egg yolks and whisk until smooth and pale. Immediately measure out 1 cup of the hot milk and slowly add it to the yolk mixture, pouring in a thin stream and whisking constantly until combined.

Turn the heat under the saucepan back up to medium and slowly add the tempered yolks, pouring in a thin stream and whisking constantly. Continue cooking and whisking until the mixture thickens to a pudding consistency and large bubbles rise to the surface, about 5 minutes. Once the bubbles appear, cook the pudding 1 to 2 more minutes, whisking constantly.

Take the saucepan off the heat and whisk in the butter and vanilla until smooth. Let the custard cool 5 minutes, or just until slightly warm, stirring often. (Don't cool it all the way or it will begin to set—if this happens, gently rewarm to remedy.)

Spoon the filling into the prepared pie shell, smoothing the top. Cover with plastic wrap, placing the wrap directly on top of the pudding surface, and chill overnight (at least 12 hours and up to 3 days) before slicing and serving.

Serve cold, each slice topped with a freshly toasted marshmallow.

granola crust

This unusual piecrust tastes just like a chewy cinnamon oatmeal granola bar. It makes a nice change from the traditional graham cracker crust. Add ½ cup ground nuts if you'd like.

MAKES 1 (9-inch / 23-cm) CRUST

2 tablespoons packed light brown sugar

½ teaspoon fine salt

1 cup / 120 g all-purpose flour

¾ cup / 75 g rolled oats

2 teaspoons ground cinnamon

1 teaspoon ground or freshly grated nutmeg

½ cup / 113 g unsalted butter, melted

Preheat the oven to 350°F (175°C) with a rack in the center.

Combine the brown sugar, salt, flour, oats, and spices in a bowl and whisk to blend. Add the melted butter and 2 tablespoons water and mix with a fork until the texture is even and the mixture gathers into a dough.

Press the dough in an even layer (about ¼ inch thick) across the bottom and up the sides of a 9-inch (23-cm) pie pan. Freeze the crust for 15 minutes before baking, or for up to 1 week (wrapped tightly in plastic).

Bake for 6 minutes, then take the pan out of the oven and use a ¼-cup measuring cup to carefully press the crust down, then return the pan to the oven and bake 6 minutes more. Transfer the pan to a wire rack and cool the crust completely to room temperature before filling, or cover the cooled crust in plastic wrap and freeze for up to 1 week.

vanilla marshmallows

Once you've eaten a homemade marshmallow, you may find you can never again bring yourself to buy the packaged ones from the supermarket. Looking for something to do with the leftovers? Try them atop steaming hot cups of cocoa—a super popular Magpie wintertime treat.

MAKES 24 (2-inch / 5-cm) SQUARES

¼ cup / 30 g cornstarch

¼ cup / 40 g confectioners' sugar

Vegetable oil or cooking spray, for coating pan and spatula

3 packets (7½ teaspoons) unflavored powdered gelatin

1 cup / 237 ml cold water, divided

1½ cups / 340 g granulated sugar

1 cup / 237 ml light corn syrup

¼ teaspoon fine salt

2 teaspoons vanilla extract

Whisk together the cornstarch and confectioners' sugar.

Lightly oil a 13 x 9 x 2-inch (33 x 23 x 5-cm) pan and dust with some of the cornstarch mixture, reserving the remainder.

In the bowl of a stand mixer, sprinkle the gelatin over ½ cup cold water and leave it to soften while you make the syrup.

In a medium saucepan, whisk together the remaining ½ cup of the cold water, sugar, and corn syrup. Bring to a boil over medium-high heat without stirring and continue cooking undisturbed until the syrup registers 240°F (115°C) on a candy or instant-read thermometer, 7 to 10 minutes.

Fit the stand mixer with the whisk attachment and turn the machine on to low speed. Slowly add the hot syrup to the gelatin mixture, pouring the syrup in a thin stream. Beat the mixture on medium-high until it is marshmallowy and cool to the touch and has nearly tripled in volume. Add the salt and vanilla, mixing on low speed until fully incorporated.

Use a rubber spatula lightly coated with vegetable oil or cooking spray to spread the marshmallow evenly in the prepared pan. Dust the top with cornstarch mixture and make sure it's completely coated and doesn't have any sticky spots. (Reserve the remaining cornstarch mixture.) Let the marshmallow set overnight before cutting.

Invert the pan onto a large cutting board. Lift up one corner of the inverted pan and use your fingers to ease the marshmallow out of the pan onto the cutting board. Use a large knife to trim the marshmallow edges straight and cut into roughly 1-inch cubes. (An oiled pizza cutter works well here, too.)

Sift the remaining cornstarch mixture into the now-empty baking pan and roll the marshmallows through it, coating all sides and shaking off excess. Transfer to an airtight container and keep at room temperature up to 1 week or freeze for 1 month.

peppermint mousse black bottom pie

This pie is a Peppermint Pattie-lover's dream: creamy chocolate-peppermint pudding beneath a cloud of airy peppermint mousse. Dress it up with peppermint candy shards for the holiday dessert table.

MAKES 1 (9-inch / 23-cm) PIE

½ recipe Magpie Dough for Flaky Piecrust (page 17), chilled overnight

4 ounces / 120 g semisweet chocolate

2½ cups / 600 ml whole milk, divided

¾ cup / 150 g granulated sugar

¼ cup / 30 g cornstarch

½ teaspoon fine salt

4 large egg yolks

2 tablespoons unsalted butter

½ teaspoon vanilla extract

½ teaspoon peppermint extract

1¼ teaspoons unflavored powdered gelatin

1 cup / 237 ml heavy cream

Chocolate shavings or crushed peppermint candies, for serving

Roll, pan, and flute the dough as directed on pages 20–23, then follow the instructions on page 24 to fully prebake the crust. Set the pan on a wire rack and let the shell cool to room temperature while you make the filling.

To make the black bottom layer, chop the chocolate and set it aside in a medium bowl.

Heat 2¼ cups of the milk in a medium saucepan over medium heat, stirring occasionally, until steaming (do not boil). Keep warm over very low heat.

Whisk together the sugar, cornstarch, and salt in a medium bowl. Add the egg yolks and continue whisking until the mixture is smooth and pale. Immediately measure out 1 cup of the hot milk and slowly whisk it into the yolk mixture, pouring in a thin stream and whisking constantly until combined.

Turn the heat under the saucepan back up to medium and slowly add the tempered yolks, pouring in a thin stream and whisking constantly. Continue cooking, whisking constantly, until the mixture thickens to a pudding consistency and a few large bubbles rise to the surface, about 5 minutes. Once the bubbles appear, continue cooking the custard, whisking constantly, for 2 more minutes.

Take the pan off the heat and whisk in the butter and the vanilla and peppermint extracts, mixing until smooth.

Measure out 1 cup of the hot custard, pour it over the chocolate, and let stand for 2 minutes, then whisk together until smooth and creamy. Pour the chocolate custard into the prepared pie shell, spreading evenly. Transfer the pan to the refrigerator to chill while you make the peppermint mousse.

To make the mousse layer, sprinkle the gelatin onto the surface of the remaining ¼ cup milk and let soften 5 minutes.

Transfer the remaining custard from the saucepan to a medium bowl and whisk in the bloomed gelatin. Refrigerate until cool, 15 to 20 minutes, whisking at 5-minute intervals to prevent the edges from setting.

In a separate clean, dry bowl, whip the cream to medium peaks (see Whipping Cream, page 130). Fold the whipped cream into the cooled custard gelatin mixture in thirds, mixing the last third just until no white streaks remain.

Retrieve the pie shell from the refrigerator. Spoon the mousse on top of the chocolate custard layer and smooth the top. Cover with plastic wrap and chill the pie overnight (at least 8 hours and up to 3 days) before slicing and serving.

Serve cold, garnished with chocolate shavings or crushed peppermint candies.

"Thin Mint" Pie: *Replace the flaky piecrust with Chocolate Cookie Crust (page 156) and top with Chocolate Cookie Crumb (page 156) instead of chocolate shavings or peppermint candies.*

eggnog cream pie

Most eggnog pies use eggnog from a carton. Our from-scratch interpretation—sweet vanilla-rum mousse in Magpie's specialty gingersnap crust—has won over countless converts from the "I'm-just-not-an-eggnog-fan" faction.

MAKES 1 (9-inch / 23-cm) PIE

1 recipe Gingersnap Crust (page 69)

2½ cups / 591 ml whole milk, divided

¾ cup / 150 g granulated sugar

¼ cup / 30 g cornstarch

¼ teaspoon fine salt

4 large egg yolks

2 tablespoons unsalted butter

½ teaspoon vanilla extract

3 tablespoons Jamaican rum (we use Appleton Estate Special Gold at the shop)

2½ teaspoons unflavored powdered gelatin

1 cup / 237 ml heavy cream

Lightly sweetened freshly whipped cream, for serving

Ground or freshly grated nutmeg, for serving

Prepare the gingersnap crust as directed on page 69. Set the pan in the refrigerator and chill the crust while you make the filling.

Heat 2¼ cups of the milk in a medium saucepan over medium heat, stirring occasionally, until steaming (don't boil!). Keep warm over very low heat.

Whisk together the sugar, cornstarch, and salt in a medium bowl. Add the egg yolks and whisk until the mixture is smooth and pale. Immediately measure out 1 cup of the hot milk and slowly add it to the yolk mixture, pouring in a thin stream and whisking constantly.

Slowly add the tempered yolks to the hot milk in the saucepan, pouring in a thin stream and whisking constantly. Turn the heat under the saucepan back up to medium and cook the mixture, whisking constantly, until it thickens to a pudding consistency and a few large bubbles rise to the surface, about 5 minutes. Once the bubbles appear, continue cooking the custard, whisking constantly, for 2 more minutes.

Remove the pan from the heat. Add the butter, vanilla extract, and rum, whisking until the custard is smooth. Transfer to a bowl and set aside to cool slightly.

Sprinkle the gelatin across the surface of the remaining ¼ cup milk and let soften 5 minutes. Whisk the bloomed gelatin into the custard and set the bowl in the refrigerator to chill until cool, 15 to 20 minutes, whisking at 5-minute intervals to prevent the edges from setting.

Whip the cream to medium peaks (see Whipping Cream, page 130) and fold it into the cooled custard in thirds, mixing the last third just until no white streaks remain.

Retrieve the gingersnap crust from the refrigerator; spoon the mousse into the prepared shell and smooth the top. Cover with plastic wrap and chill the pie overnight (at least 12 hours or up to 3 days) before slicing and serving.

Serve cold with whipped cream and a light sprinkling of nutmeg.

PIE MILKSHAKE

Love ice cream with your pie? Try a pie milkshake. It's a simple and deliciously different way to enjoy pie à la mode! My all-time favorite slices for pie shakes include: Coffee-Chocolate-Cinnamon Pecan (page 179), Café Mocha (page 139), Plum Cherry Almond Crumb (page 116), Peach Lattice Pie with Bourbon Caramel (page 93), Blueberry Cardamom Pie with Polenta Streusel (page 88), Nutter Butter (see Spin, page 138), Chocolate Blackout (page 163), Peppermint Mousse Black Bottom (page 170), Oatmeal Cookie (page 150), and Butterscotch Bourbon (page 160).

MAKES 1 (16-ounce) SHAKE

1 slice of the pie of your choice, cut into 1-inch pieces

1½ cups / 283 g good-quality vanilla ice cream

6 tablespoons / 93 ml whole milk

Combine the ice cream and milk in a blender and process on high speed until smooth. Add the pie chunks, crust and all, to the blender and pulse 5 to 10 times, depending on how chunky a milkshake you're after. Pour into a tall glass and serve with a wide straw and a long spoon. If it's a pie with a special topping (bourbon caramel; cookie, cake, or other crumble; candy bits; chocolate curls; pretzel crunch and so forth), by all means, add some of that on top.

shoofly pie

Shoofly à la Magpie is "wet bottom" style—with a gooey bottom and cakey top layer—and aromatic with cinnamon, ginger, and black pepper. Back home, everyone has their own preference for how to have their shoofly—from heated up and topped with a scoop of vanilla ice cream to room temperature with a cold glass of milk or a hot cup of coffee. Go with whatever suits you.

MAKES 1 (9-inch / 23-cm) PIE

½ recipe Magpie Dough for Flaky Piecrust (page 17), chilled overnight

1 cup / 124 g all-purpose flour

¾ cup / 144 g packed light brown sugar

1 teaspoon ground cinnamon

1 teaspoon ground ginger

⅛ teaspoon freshly ground black pepper

⅛ teaspoon fine salt

2 tablespoons unsalted butter, at room temperature

½ cup / 118 ml mild molasses

½ cup / 118 ml dark corn syrup

1 large egg, beaten

1 teaspoon baking soda

Roll, pan, and flute the dough as directed on page 20–23. Set the pan in the refrigerator and chill the shell while you make the filling.

Preheat the oven to 375°F (190°C) with a rack in the center. Line a rimmed baking sheet with parchment paper.

Whisk the flour, brown sugar, cinnamon, ginger, black pepper, and salt together in a medium bowl. Add the butter, and use your hands to blend until the mixture resembles coarse cornmeal. Measure out ¼ cup and reserve for the crumb topping. Add the molasses, dark corn syrup, and egg into the mixture remaining in the bowl, whisking until well combined.

Bring a small kettle of water to a boil. Use a heatproof measuring cup to measure out 1 cup (240 ml) of the boiling water.

Slowly add ¾ cup of the water to the molasses mixture, pouring in a thin stream and whisking to combine.

Add the baking soda to the ¼ cup water remaining in the measuring cup and stir until dissolved. Whisk the baking soda mixture into the molasses mixture and stir until uniformly incorporated and smooth.

Retrieve the chilled shell from the refrigerator and set the pan on the parchment-lined baking sheet. Carefully pour the molasses filling into the pie shell. Sprinkle the reserved crumb mixture evenly across the top. Transfer the baking sheet to the oven and bake the pie 10 minutes, then rotate the pie, lower the oven temperature to 350°F (175°C), and bake 35 to 40 minutes more, or until the filling is puffed and set.

Transfer the baking sheet to a wire rack and let the pie cool completely to room temperature. Slice and serve, or cover with plastic wrap and keep at room temperature for up to 3 days. Before serving, rewarm 5 to 10 minutes in a 350°F (175°C) oven, if desired.

coffee-chocolate-cinnamon pecan pie

Pecan pie can be awfully sweet. Magpie's rendition of this classic retains the beloved sticky goo but incorporates coffee, cinnamon, and bittersweet chocolate to dial down the cloying sweetness and emphasize the euphoric flavor of the pecans.

MAKES 1 (9-inch / 23-cm) PIE

½ recipe Magpie Dough for Flaky Piecrust (page 17), chilled overnight

1 cup / 237 ml light corn syrup

½ cup / 110 g packed light brown sugar

3 tablespoons unsalted butter, melted and cooled

3 large eggs, at room temperature

1 teaspoon instant espresso powder

1 teaspoon vanilla extract

1 teaspoon ground cinnamon

½ teaspoon fine salt

1½ cups / 150 g pecan halves or pieces

3 ounces / 90 g bittersweet chocolate (60% cacao), coarsely chopped

Vanilla ice cream or Maple Bourbon Ice Cream (page 124), for serving

Roll, pan, and flute the dough (pages 20–23), then parbake the crust (page 24). Set the pan on a wire rack and cool the shell completely to room temperature.

Preheat the oven to 400°F (200°C) with a rack in the center. Line a rimmed baking sheet with parchment paper.

Combine the corn syrup and brown sugar in a large bowl and beat together with an electric mixer on medium-high speed until smooth and creamy, about 3 minutes.

Slowly beat in the butter, then add the eggs one at a time and beat until smooth and foamy, about 3 minutes.

(Continued)

Beat in the espresso powder, vanilla, cinnamon, and salt and continue blending until the mixture is thick and frothy.

Rap the bowl against the counter a couple of times to pop any bubbles that might have formed beneath the surface. (Otherwise the bubbles can rise and burst during baking and cause pockmarking across the top of the filling.)

Set the pie pan on the parchment-lined baking sheet. Layer the pecans and chocolate across the bottom of the cooled parbaked crust. Top with the filling, spreading evenly.

Transfer the baking sheet to the oven and bake the pie at 400°F (200°C) for 15 minutes, then rotate the pie, lower the oven temperature to 350°F (175°C), and bake another 20 to 25 minutes, or until the middle and the edges of the filling are puffed and the top is beautifully browned and no longer jiggles when tapped.

Set the pan on a wire rack and cool the pie completely to room temperature. Cover with plastic wrap and let sit at room temperature overnight (at least 12 hours and up to 3 days) before cutting and serving with vanilla or maple bourbon ice cream.

Note: At the shop we've found that chilling the pie before slicing with a serrated knife makes it easier to get nice tidy slices.

whiskey walnut pie

Also known as Kentucky Bourbon Pie, Derby Pie, Bluegrass Pie, and Thoroughbred Pie, bourbon chocolate nut pies are a hallowed Southern tradition. To come up with a Magpie rendition of this classic, we played around with all sorts of different approaches before we came up with one we really liked. Orange bitters bring a hint of citrus that complements the bourbon and melds especially well with bittersweet chocolate; walnuts, with their slight bitterness and firm crunch, won out over the more commonly used pecans. Customers go cuckoo for it—we sell out of this pie on a daily basis whenever we put it on the menu.

MAKES 1 (9-inch / 23-cm) PIE

½ recipe Magpie Dough for Flaky Piecrust (page 17), chilled overnight

3 ounces / 85 g bittersweet chocolate (60% cacao), coarsely chopped

½ cup / 113 g unsalted butter

3 tablespoons bourbon

1 cup / 192 g granulated sugar

½ cup / 115 g packed light brown sugar

¾ teaspoon fine salt

2 tablespoons cornstarch

2 large eggs, at room temperature

1 large egg yolk

3 teaspoons vanilla extract

1 teaspoon orange bitters (optional)

1½ cups / 150 g walnuts, toasted and coarsely chopped

Roll, pan, and flute the dough as directed on pages 20–23, then follow the instructions on page 24 to parbake the piecrust. Set the pan on a wire rack and cool the shell to room temperature before you make the filling.

Preheat the oven to 300°F (150°C) with a rack in the center. Line a rimmed baking sheet with parchment paper.

Spread the chocolate in an even layer across the bottom of the parbaked, cooled pie shell. Bake for 5 minutes, then take the pan out of the oven, use an offset spatula to spread the melted chocolate, and set the pie shell aside.

(Continued)

Bring the butter to a simmer in a medium saucepan. Remove the pan from the heat and slowly whisk in the bourbon. Set aside to cool slightly.

Whisk the sugars, salt, and cornstarch together in a large bowl. Add the whole eggs, egg yolk, vanilla, and bitters (if using) and beat with the whisk until smooth, about 3 minutes. Slowly add the warm bourbon butter, pouring in a thin stream and whisking constantly for 1 to 2 minutes. Continue mixing until the ingredients are uniformly incorporated and the mixture is bubbly across the top, 2 to 3 minutes. Fold in the walnuts.

Set the pie pan on the parchment-lined baking sheet. Scoop the filling into the chocolate-lined pie shell, spreading evenly. Carefully transfer the baking sheet to the oven and bake the pie 30 to 40 minutes, or until the top is golden brown, the edges are set, and the center jiggles slightly.

Set the pan on a wire rack and cool the pie completely to room temperature. Cover with plastic wrap and let sit at room temperature overnight (at least 12 hours and up to 3 days) before cutting and serving.

Note: At the shop, we've found that chilling the pie before slicing with a serrated knife makes it easier to get nice, tidy slices.

banana nilla pudding pie

Here's a fusion of two classic comfort foods—banana pudding and banana cream pie. Adding Nilla Wafers puts a special little twist on things and also serves a practical purpose: The cookies and banana slices are sandwiched together and embedded in the filling to help prevent the bananas from turning brown and slimy. The cookie softens up and adds a nice third texture to the pie.

◆ MAKES 1 (9-inch / 23-cm) PIE ◆

½ recipe Magpie Dough for Flaky Piecrust (page 17), chilled overnight

½ cup / 118 ml evaporated milk

2 cups / 473 ml whole milk

½ cup plus 2 tablespoons / 130 g granulated sugar

¼ cup / 30 g cornstarch

¼ teaspoon fine salt

¼ teaspoon ground or freshly grated nutmeg

5 large egg yolks

2 tablespoons unsalted butter, at room temperature

1 teaspoon Jamaican rum (we use Appleton Estate Special Gold at the shop)

1 teaspoon vanilla extract

1 teaspoon banana extract

1 banana, peeled and cut into ¼-inch-thick rounds

22 Nilla Wafers, plus 8 more for serving

Lightly sweetened freshly whipped cream, for serving

Roll, pan, and flute the dough as directed on pages 20–23, then follow the instructions on page 24 to fully prebake the piecrust. Set the pan on a wire rack and let the shell cool to room temperature while you make the filling.

To make the filling, combine the evaporated milk and whole milk in a medium saucepan and cook over medium heat, stirring occasionally, until steaming. Keep warm over very low heat.

Combine the sugar, cornstarch, salt, and nutmeg in a medium bowl and whisk together. Add the egg yolks and whisk until the mixture is smooth and pale. Immediately measure out 1 cup of the hot milk

(Continued)

mixture and slowly add it to the yolk mixture, pouring in a thin stream and whisking constantly until combined.

Turn the heat under the saucepan back up to medium. Slowly add the tempered yolks to the saucepan, pouring in a thin stream and whisking constantly over medium heat. Continue cooking, whisking constantly, until the mixture thickens to a pudding consistency and a few large bubbles rise to the surface, 5 to 7 minutes. Once the bubbles appear, continue cooking the pudding, whisking constantly, for 2 more minutes.

Remove the saucepan from the heat and whisk in the butter, rum, vanilla, and banana extract, whisking until smooth. Set the pudding aside to cool for 5 minutes.

To assemble the pie, spoon half of the filling into the prepared shell and top with a single layer of 11 wafers, flat-sides up. Top each wafer with a banana slice, followed by another wafer flat-side down. Gently press the cookie sandwiches down into the filling. Spoon the remaining pudding into the pie shell and smooth the top. Cover with plastic wrap, pressing onto the surface of the pudding, and chill overnight (at least 12 hours or up to 3 days) before slicing and serving.

Serve cold, with whipped cream and a Nilla Wafer.

Vanilla Nilla Pie: Omit the bananas and banana extract. Spoon one-third of the filling into the prepared shell, spread evenly, and top with 11 wafers. Then spoon in another third of the filling and top with the remaining 11 wafers. Top with the remaining filling. Smooth top, press plastic wrap directly onto the filling surface, and chill overnight (at least 12 hours and up to 3 days) before slicing and serving.

chocolate pillow puff pie

Pillowy chocolate mousse perfection, topped with a dreamy cloud of homemade marshmallow puff, this pie is best when served chilled. A shot of coffee in the mousse filling enhances the deep chocolate flavor.

◄ MAKES 1 (9-inch / 23-cm) PIE ►

½ recipe Magpie Dough for Flaky Piecrust (page 17), chilled overnight

¼ cup / 59 ml brewed coffee, cooled

4 tablespoons unsalted butter, divided

8 ounces / 226 g bittersweet chocolate (60% cacao), chopped

3 large eggs, separated

1 teaspoon vanilla extract

Pinch fine salt

1 teaspoon unflavored powdered gelatin

¼ teaspoon cream of tartar

⅓ cup / 64 g granulated sugar

½ cup / 118 ml cold heavy cream

Marshmallow Puff (page 188), for serving

Chocolate shavings, for serving

Roll, pan, and flute the dough as directed on pages 20–23, then fully pre-bake the piecrust as directed on page 24. Set the pan on a wire rack and let the shell cool to room temperature while you make the filling.

Combine the coffee and ½ cup water in a medium saucepan over low heat and whisk in 2 tablespoons of the butter until melted. Remove from the heat, add the chocolate, shake the pan gently to distribute the chocolate so that the liquid covers it all, and let stand 1 to 2 minutes. Whisk until completely smooth, then whisk in the remaining 2 tablespoons butter. Cool slightly.

Whisk the egg yolks into the chocolate mixture one at a time. Set the saucepan over low heat and cook the mixture, whisking constantly, for 3 to 4 minutes, or until glossy.

Remove the pan from the heat and whisk in the vanilla and salt. Transfer the mixture to a large bowl and let cool to room temperature, whisking often to keep it smooth.

Put ½ cup water in a small saucepan, sprinkle the gelatin on top, and let sit 5 minutes to soften. Set the pan over low heat and stir until the gelatin is completely dissolved, 1 to 2 minutes.

Whisk the gelatin mixture into the cooled chocolate mixture. Refrigerate, whisking every 5 minutes, until mixture resembles a fudge sauce, about 10 to 15 minutes total. (Warning: Don't let it sit any longer, or the gelatin will set; if it does set, gently re-soften in a double boiler.)

Use a stand mixer to beat the egg whites and cream of tartar to soft peaks (see Whipping Egg Whites, page 132). Gradually add the sugar, mixing on high speed until thick, glossy, and firm, 5 to 7 minutes.

Fold one-third of the meringue into the chocolate mixture. Gently fold in the rest of the meringue and continue folding until no white streaks remain.

Wash and dry the beaters or whisk attachment, and in a clean, dry bowl, whip the cream to medium peaks (see Whipping Cream, page 130). Fold the whipped cream into the chocolate mixture until no white streaks remain.

Scoop the mousse into the prebaked pie shell and smooth the top. Cover with plastic wrap and chill overnight (at least 12 hours or up to 3 days) before slicing and serving with a big dollop of marshmallow puff and chocolate shavings atop each slice.

Note: This recipe includes uncooked egg white, but you can use pasteurized instead (because of the slight risk of salmonella, raw eggs should not be served to the very young, the ill or elderly, or to pregnant women).

marshmallow puff

The homemade version of this confection is way better than store-bought—and downright impossible to resist.

◄■ **MAKES ABOUT 3 CUPS** ■►

¾ cup / 144 g granulated sugar

½ cup / 120 g light corn syrup

Pinch fine salt

2 large egg whites

¼ teaspoon cream of tartar

1½ teaspoons vanilla extract

Whisk the sugar, corn syrup, and salt together with ¼ cup water in a small saucepan. Bring the mixture to a boil undisturbed over medium-high heat and continue boiling, without stirring, until the temperature reaches 240°F (115°C) on a candy thermometer.

Meanwhile, as the syrup heats, use a stand mixer fitted with the whisk attachment to beat the egg whites and cream of tartar to soft peaks (see Whipping Egg Whites, page 130).

Turn the mixer speed to low and slowly pour in the hot syrup, taking care not to let the syrup hit the side of the bowl (which will cause it to harden and adhere to the bowl). Add the vanilla, turn the mixer speed back up to medium-high, and whip until the puff is doubled in size and glossy and the bottom of the bowl is cool to the touch, 8 to 10 minutes.

The puff can be kept in an airtight container in the refrigerator for up to 2 weeks or frozen up to 1 month.

cookie dough hand pies

These are diabolically delicious, a rapid-fire sellout whenever we put them on the menu. The filling is based on a classic chocolate chip cookie dough, minus the leavening and milk instead of eggs—we found that these two adaptations were key to creating a filling that stays soft and doughy when baked inside a pastry pocket.

MAKES 8 (4-inch / 10-cm) HAND PIES

1 recipe Magpie Dough for Flaky Piecrust (page 17), chilled overnight

1 stick / 113 g unsalted butter, at room temperature

¾ cup / 75 g packed light brown sugar

2 teaspoons vanilla extract

½ teaspoon fine salt

1 cup / 125 g all-purpose flour

2 tablespoons / 30 g whole milk

1 cup /175 g semisweet chocolate chips

1 large egg yolk

Kosher salt and coarse sugar, for sprinkling

Follow the directions on pages 40–41 to roll, cut, and chill the rounds of pie dough. While the rounds are chilling, make the filling.

Beat the butter and the sugar together until creamy. Add the vanilla and salt and continue mixing. Add the flour and mix to combine, scraping down the sides of the bowl. Add the milk and continue mixing until smooth. Use a flexible rubber a spatula to gently fold in the chocolate chips.

Preheat the oven to 400°F (200°C) with a rack in the center. Line a rimmed baking sheet with parchment paper.

Retrieve the dough rounds from the refrigerator. Whisk the egg yolk together with 1 tablespoon water. Lightly brush the edges of the dough circles with the egg wash. Divide the filling among the eight circles, about 3 tablespoons filling each. Fold the dough over the filling and press the edges together. Use a fork to gently press the edges to seal and crimp.

Set the hand pies on the parchment-lined baking sheet. Transfer the baking sheet to the refrigerator and chill the pies for 15 minutes. Lightly brush the tops of the pies with egg wash and sprinkle with a little kosher salt and coarse sugar. Use a small sharp knife to cut a small slit in the top of each pie.

Bake the chilled hand pies for 22 to 25 minutes, or until the crusts are golden brown, rotating the baking sheet halfway through the baking time. Let the hand pies cool for 15 minutes before serving.

quiches, potpies, *and* other savories

IT'S BEEN SAID THAT ANYTHING CAN BE TURNED INTO A PIE. CALL ME BIASED, BUT I'D SAY THAT'S A TRUTH TO LIVE BY—ESPECIALLY WHEN IT COMES TO SAVORY PIES.

Food historians say that pie originated as a means of serving up various quasi-edible odds and ends, putting them in a crust that, in the early days, was more a hard, portable container than something to be savored. There are even those who say "pie" might be an abbreviated reference to—yes, indeed—the magpie, the bird that gathers a variety of things. That's not a factoid I had on hand when I opened the shop, but there you go!

A good piecrust can hold anything you want to put in it. And I have a lot of fun putting all sorts of savory things in our piecrust: macaroni and cheese (page 213), spaghetti and marinara (page 228), cheeseburger (page 218), and Croque Monsieur (page 202).

From day one, the savory menu at Magpie has had certain tendencies. You can take me out of the south-central Pennsylvania countryside, but twenty-plus years and a bunch of culinary training later, there is still no taking the country out of my cooking. Magpie mains are warm-your-belly fare, whether derived from dishes I grew up on (like Ham Loaf Pie, page 220, and Chicken Corn Pie, page 246) or inspired by classical dishes (like Quiche Lorraine, page 193).

I love to take classic comfort foods, go artisanal with the presentation, add a little fun, and keep things homey. The potpies, for example, are in lovely cylindrical, hand-hewn pastry shells. They're filled with warm, hearty, made-from-scratch filling, and topped with something tasty that adds another, complementary element. So Chicken Potpie (page 230) is crowned with a fluffy, super savory Cheddar Biscuit (page 232);

Macaroni and Cheese Potpie (page 213) has zesty, crispy Old Bay Cheez-It Crunch (page 214); there's a silky layer of Cauliflower Mash (page 225) atop the Shepherd's Potpie (page 223); and nuggets of chive crumble (page 245) top the Seafood Chowder Potpies (page 243).

And there's some good fun to be had with Magpie quiches—as elegant as they may be, just by virtue of height and their soufflé-like filling. Jalapeño Bacon "Popper" Quiche (page 196), anyone? (And just because it's drop-dead gorgeous doesn't mean a Magpie quiche isn't super adaptable. See page 200 for a guide to creating your own signature quiche.

Growing up, when the garden between our house and my grandparents' was bountiful with tomatoes, squash, and corn, we would make summer savory pies, perfect to take to a picnic or give to a neighbor. Nowadays at the shop, the Magpie menu features an ever-changing array of seasonal specialties that owe a lot to those back-home dishes made with backyard produce: Tomato Cheddar Corn Pie (page 204), Summer Squash Pie (page 207), and Smoked Gouda Butternut Squash Pie (page 215), to name a few.

This chapter starts with Magpie breakfast and brunch fare: quiches and other pies we serve morning through noontime (also see Breakfast Oatmeal Pie, page 135). The rest of the chapter is devoted to the greatest hits from our dinner lineup. Just in case it doesn't go without saying: breakfast for dinner is a beautiful thing.

quiche lorraine

Lorraine, the quintessence of quiche—bacon, onion, eggs, and milk baked up in a simple and perfectly savory tart. Our own version of this venerable classic is, like all Magpie quiches, baked in a springform pan for airy, soufflé-like height. It makes for a brilliant brunch any time of year.

MAKES 1 (9-inch / 23-cm) QUICHE

1 recipe Magpie Dough for Flaky Piecrust (page 17), chilled overnight

2 tablespoons cornstarch

1½ cups / 355 ml whole milk

2 cups / 473 ml heavy cream

10 large eggs

1½ teaspoons granulated garlic

1½ teaspoons granulated onion

¼ teaspoon red pepper flakes

¾ teaspoon kosher salt

½ teaspoon freshly ground black pepper

2 teaspoons dry mustard

1 tablespoon unsalted butter

1 small yellow onion, diced

4 ounces / 113 g diced Canadian bacon

1½ cups / 170 g grated Swiss cheese

1 tablespoon fresh thyme leaves, minced

Roll, pan, and bake the quiche shell as directed on pages 38–39. Set the pan on a wire rack and let the shell cool to room temperature while you make the filling.

Preheat the oven to 375°F (190°C) with a rack in the center. Line a rimmed baking sheet with parchment paper.

To make the custard filling, put the cornstarch in a large mixing bowl and whisk in the milk until the cornstarch is dissolved and incorporated. Whisk in the heavy cream, eggs, granulated garlic and onion, red pepper flakes, salt and pepper, and dry mustard, mixing until well combined.

(Continued)

Melt the butter in a medium sauté pan over medium heat. Add the onions to the pan and cook until soft, about 5 to 7 minutes. Add the Canadian bacon and cook until golden, about 5 minutes more. Set the mixture aside to cool slightly.

To assemble the quiche, set the springform pan on the prepared baking sheet and spread half of the cheese evenly across the bottom of the pastry shell. Layer in the onion and bacon mixture and sprinkle on the thyme. Top with the remaining cheese and slowly pour the custard over top.

Carefully transfer the baking sheet to the oven and bake the quiche about 75 to 90 minutes, or until the custard is firm around the edges but still quite jiggly in the center (you can confirm for certain with an instant-read thermometer, which will register 160°F / 70°C when the custard is done), rotating halfway through the baking time.

Set the pan on a wire rack and cool until warm, about 1 hour, before removing the springform ring and cutting and serving the quiche.

Serve warm or at room temperature.

Lorraine with Spinach, Sun-Dried Tomato, and Peas: Add the following to the cooked bacon and onions: 1 cup cooked, drained, chopped spinach; ½ cup minced sun-dried tomatoes; and ¼ to ½ cup thawed petite peas. Bake about 90 minutes.

jalapeño bacon "popper" quiche

Popular party foods aside, the central inspiration for this quiche is the simple fact that hot sauce and eggs are incredibly delicious together.

◄ **MAKES 1 (9-inch / 23-cm) QUICHE** ►

1 recipe Magpie Dough for
Flaky Piecrust (page 17),
chilled overnight

2 tablespoons cornstarch

1½ cups / 355 ml whole milk

2 cups / 473 ml heavy cream

10 large eggs

1½ teaspoons granulated garlic

1½ teaspoons granulated onion

¼ teaspoon red pepper flakes

¾ teaspoon kosher salt

½ teaspoon freshly ground
black pepper

1½ cups / 170 g grated sharp
Cheddar cheese

½ cup drained pickled jalapeño slices

5 slices bacon, cooked, drained,
and coarsely chopped

4 ounces / 113 g cream cheese,
cut into ½-inch cubes

Follow the instructions on pages 38–39 to roll, pan, and bake the quiche shell. Set the pan on a wire rack and leave the shell to cool while you prepare the filling.

Preheat the oven to 375°F (190°C) with a rack in the center. Line a rimmed baking sheet with parchment paper.

To make the custard filling, put the cornstarch in a large mixing bowl and whisk in the milk and heavy cream until the cornstarch is dissolved and incorporated. Whisk in the eggs, granulated garlic and onion, red pepper flakes, salt, and pepper, mixing until well combined. Set aside.

To assemble the quiche, set the springform pan on the prepared baking sheet. Scatter the grated cheese evenly across the bottom of the shell, followed by the jalapeños, bacon, and cream cheese. Slowly pour the custard over top.

Carefully transfer the baking sheet to the oven and bake the quiche 75 to 90 minutes, or until the custard is firm around the edges but the center still jiggles loosely (you can confirm for certain with an instant-read thermometer, which will register 160°F / 70°C when the custard is done), rotating halfway through the baking time. Set the pan on a wire rack and cool until warm, about 1 hour, before removing the springform ring and cutting and serving the quiche.

Serve warm or at room temperature.

Cherry Pepper "Popper" Quiche: Swap in pickled sweet or hot cherry peppers for the jalapeños, provolone for the cream cheese, and prosciutto for the bacon.

herb goat cheese quiche

This is an elegant, picture-perfect quiche. The combination of goat cheese and herbs makes the filling deliciously fluffy and fragrant. It suits any season, and always pairs well with a simple green salad; in summer, it is especially delectable with a fresh tomato salad.

MAKES 1 (9-inch / 23-cm) QUICHE

1 recipe Magpie Dough for Flaky Piecrust (page 17), chilled overnight

2 tablespoons cornstarch

1½ cups / 355 ml whole milk

2 cups / 473 ml heavy cream

10 large eggs

1½ teaspoons granulated garlic

1½ teaspoons granulated onion

¼ teaspoon red pepper flakes

¾ teaspoon kosher salt

½ teaspoon freshly ground black pepper

1½ cups / 170 g grated Monterey Jack cheese

3 tablespoons chopped fresh basil leaves

2 teaspoons chopped fresh thyme leaves

2 to 3 scallions, finely sliced (white and green parts)

4 ounces / 113 g soft mild goat cheese

Follow the instructions on pages 38–39 to roll, pan, and bake the quiche shell. Set the pan on a wire rack and leave the shell to cool while you prepare the filling.

Preheat the oven to 375°F (190°C) with a rack in the center. Line a rimmed baking sheet with parchment paper.

To make the custard filling, put the cornstarch in a large mixing bowl and whisk in the milk and heavy cream until the cornstarch is dissolved and incorporated. Whisk in the eggs, granulated garlic and onion, red pepper flakes, salt, and pepper, mixing until well combined. Set aside.

To assemble the quiche, set the springform pan on the prepared baking sheet. Scatter the grated cheese across the bottom of the shell, followed by the herbs and scallions. Use your fingers to crumble the goat cheese over the herbs. Slowly pour the custard over top.

Carefully transfer the baking sheet to the oven and bake the quiche 75 to 90 minutes, or until the custard is firm around the edges but the center still jiggles when you shake the pan (you can confirm for certain with an instant-read thermometer, which will register 160°F / 70°C when the custard is done), rotating halfway through the baking time. Set the pan on a wire rack and cool until warm, about 1 hour, before removing the springform ring and cutting and serving the quiche.

Serve warm or at room temperature.

Camembert Herb Quiche: *Substitute Camembert for the goat cheese, and use tarragon, parsley, and chives in place of the basil, thyme, and scallions.*

QUICHE À LA MAGPIE

Here is the formula we use to create our quiches. It's fairly straightforward, and you can make the process quicker and easier if you do some advance prep: bake the shell (cool it to room temperature in the pan, double-wrap, and freeze for up to 2 months); whisk together your custard (cover and refrigerate overnight); grate the cheese; and sauté the other fillings you've selected. Then, a few hours before you want to serve the quiche, fill the shell as directed in the recipe below, ease the brimming pan into oven, and spend the next hour or so savoring the aroma that emanates from your kitchen. Flip the oven light on now and then to marvel as the filling metamorphoses from viscous liquid to fluffy splendor. Prepare for applause—and an absolutely delicious meal.

◇ **MAKES 1 (9-inch / 23-cm) QUICHE** ◇

1 prebaked Quiche Shell (page 38)

2 tablespoons cornstarch

1½ cups / 355 ml whole milk

2 cups / 473 ml heavy cream

10 large eggs

1½ teaspoons granulated garlic

1½ teaspoons granulated onion

¼ teaspoon red pepper flakes

¾ teaspoon kosher salt

½ teaspoon freshly ground black pepper

1½ cups grated cheese, divided

OPTIONAL ADD-INS:

1 onion, chopped and sautéed

2 cups vegetables, cooked (steer clear of very wet veggies, such as tomatoes)

8 ounces cured or cooked and drained meat (such as salami, pepperoni, ham, bacon, ground beef, loose sausage)

1 tablespoon minced fresh herbs

Preheat the oven to 375°F (190°C). Line a large rimmed baking sheet with parchment paper.

To make the custard, put the cornstarch in a large mixing bowl. Pour in the milk and heavy cream and whisk the mixture until the cornstarch is dissolved. Whisk in the eggs and dry seasonings until well combined.

Set the prebaked pastry shell (still in the springform) on the parchment-lined baking sheet. Sprinkle half the cheese across the bottom of the shell, and follow with whatever vegetables, meat, and herbs you've decided to include. Top with the remaining cheese, then slowly pour in the custard.

Carefully slide the baking sheet into the oven, and bake the quiche for 75 to 90 minutes, or until the custard is firmly set at the edges but is still jiggly in the middle, rotating halfway through the baking time. (A skewer inserted in the center should come out clean; an instant-read thermometer should register 160°F / 70°C.)

Transfer the baking sheet to a wire rack and let the quiche cool for 1 hour before carefully removing the springform ring and cutting and serving.

Serve warm or at room temperature.

A few favorite Magpie combos: broccoli rabe, smoked sun-dried tomatoes, and mozzarella; Italian sausage, leeks, and thyme; spinach, goat cheese, and roasted red peppers.

Note: The entire shebang can be done as a make-ahead: Prebake the quiche up to 3 days ahead and cool to room temperature; leave it in the springform and wrap it in aluminum foil and refrigerate; rewarm, in the foil, in a 350°F / 175°C oven for 20 to 25 minutes, or until warmed through.

croque monsieur pie

Inspired by the classic French sandwich, this pie is terrific to serve for brunch with a seasonal green salad. It's also a great make-ahead and keeps very well for at least 3 days after baking. Do be sure to get acquainted with Madame as well (see Spin on this recipe).

MAKES 1 (9-inch / 23-cm) PIE

½ recipe Magpie Dough for Flaky Piecrust (page 17), chilled overnight

2 large eggs

1 (12-ounce / 340-ml) can evaporated milk

¼ teaspoon hot sauce

1 teaspoon fine salt

¼ teaspoon freshly ground black pepper

1 tablespoon dry mustard

1¼ cups / 142 g grated Gruyère cheese, divided

1¼ cups / 142 g grated Munster cheese, divided

½ loaf (8 ounces / 226 g) Italian bread, baguette, or other light bakery bread, cut into 1-inch cubes and lightly toasted

6 ounces / 170 g Black Forest deli-sliced ham, cut into ½-inch-wide strips

1 tablespoon chopped chives

Roll, pan, and flute the dough as directed on pages 20–23, then follow the instructions on page 24 to parbake the crust. Set the pan on a wire rack, and leave the shell to cool while you make the filling.

Whisk together the eggs, evaporated milk, hot sauce, salt, pepper, and dry mustard in a large mixing bowl. Add 1 cup of the Gruyère and 1 cup of the Munster, and mix to combine. Add the toasted bread cubes and toss to coat the cubes thoroughly with the egg mixture. Set the bowl aside for 20 minutes to allow the bread to absorb the custard.

Preheat the oven to 375°F (190°C) with a rack in the center. Line a rimmed baking sheet with parchment paper.

Add the sliced ham and chives to the custard and bread mixture, stirring to combine.

Set the prepared pie shell on the parchment-lined baking sheet. Pour the filling into the shell and spread evenly. Sprinkle the top of the pie with the remaining Munster and Gruyère.

Carefully transfer the baking sheet to the oven and bake the pie for 45 to 55 minutes, or until the top is a beautiful golden brown and the custard is set (the tip of a knife inserted in the center comes out clean), rotating halfway through the baking time.

Let the pie rest 10 minutes before slicing and serving.

Croque Madame: *Top each slice with a sunny side-up fried egg.*

tomato cheddar corn pie

This pie is a favorite Magpie menu item for that fleeting month or so when local tomatoes and corn are both at their peak of deliciousness. Nothing tastes more like summer.

◄ MAKES 1 (9-inch / 23-cm) PIE ►

½ recipe Magpie Dough for Flaky Piecrust (page 17), chilled overnight

1 tablespoon unsalted butter

2 garlic cloves, minced

2 cups / 250 g fresh sweet corn kernels (from 2 large ears)

½ teaspoon kosher salt, plus more for seasoning corn and tomatoes

¼ teaspoon freshly ground black pepper, plus more for seasoning corn and tomatoes

½ cup / 118 ml heavy cream

2 large eggs, beaten

½ teaspoon red pepper flakes

½ teaspoon granulated garlic

1 teaspoon cornstarch

1½ cups / 170 g grated sharp white Cheddar cheese, divided

3 scallions, finely sliced (green and white parts), divided

¼ cup / 25 g chopped fresh basil leaves, divided

4 plum tomatoes, seeded, sliced ¼ inch thick, and drained on paper towels

Roll, pan, and flute the dough as directed on pages 20–23, then par-bake the crust as directed on page 24. Set the pan on a wire rack and let the shell cool while you prepare the filling.

Preheat the oven to 350°F (175°C) with a rack in the center. Line a rimmed baking sheet with parchment paper.

Melt the butter in a medium sauté pan over medium heat. Add the garlic to the pan and cook just until fragrant, about 1 minute. Stir in the corn and a pinch each of salt and pepper and cook for 5 to 8 minutes, or until the corn is tender and fragrant. Set aside to cool.

(Continued)

Whisk together the cream, eggs, red pepper, granulated garlic, cornstarch, ½ teaspoon kosher salt, and ¼ teaspoon black pepper in a mixing bowl.

To assemble the pie, set the parbaked pie shell on the prepared baking sheet. Spread half of the grated cheese evenly across the bottom of the crust. Layer on the corn mixture, followed by half of the scallions and half of the basil. Top with the tomato slices, arranging them in a circle pattern, edges overlapping. Sprinkle the tomatoes with salt and pepper. Top the tomatoes with the remaining cheese, scallions, and basil. Pour in the egg mixture *slowly and evenly* (to preserve the placement of the tomatoes).

Carefully transfer the baking sheet to the oven and bake the pie 50 to 60 minutes, or until the top is golden brown and the custard is nearly set, rotating halfway through the baking time.

Cool 10 minutes before slicing and serving.

summer squash pie

Growing up in small-town PA, my family and all of our neighbors had backyard gardens for growing tomatoes, cucumbers, peppers, green beans, and all kinds of summer squash—pattypan, crookneck, yellow squash, and zucchini, to name a few. This pie is a great way to do something a little different with an abundance of whatever kind of summer squash you might grow in your garden or pick up at your local farmer's market.

MAKES 1 (9-inch / 23-cm) PIE

½ recipe Magpie Dough for Flaky Piecrust (page 17), chilled overnight

2 tablespoons unsalted butter

1½ pounds / 680 g summer squash, thinly sliced

1 small yellow onion, thinly sliced

2 garlic cloves, minced

1 teaspoon fresh thyme leaves, minced

1 teaspoon fresh tarragon leaves, minced

½ teaspoon fine salt

¼ teaspoon freshly ground black pepper

2 large eggs

¼ cup / 60 g heavy cream

2 tablespoons Dijon mustard

½ cup / 40 g grated Monterey Jack cheese, divided

¼ cup / 25 g grated Parmesan cheese, divided

Roll, pan, and flute the dough as directed on pages 20–23, then follow the directions on page 24 to parbake the crust. Set the pan on a wire rack and let the shell cool to room temperature.

Preheat the oven to 375°F (190°C) with a rack in the center. Line a rimmed baking sheet with parchment paper.

Melt the butter in a large skillet over medium-high heat, then add the squash and onions and sauté until the onions begin to soften, 5 to 7 minutes. Stir in the garlic and continue sautéing another 5 minutes. Take the pan off the heat and stir in the fresh herbs and the salt and pepper.

(Continued)

In a small bowl, whisk together the eggs, cream, and Dijon mustard.

Set the parbaked shell on the parchment-lined baking sheet. Sprinkle half the Jack and half the Parmesan across the bottom of the shell. Spoon the squash mixture in an even layer over the cheeses, then sprinkle on the remaining cheese. Pour the egg mixture evenly over the pie.

Transfer the baking sheet to the oven and bake the pie 25 to 30 minutes, or until golden and set, rotating the sheet halfway through the baking time.

Cool 10 minutes before slicing and serving.

ham-leek-dijon potpies

This is a wonderful way to use ham left over from a holiday dinner.

◆ **MAKES 8 (4-inch / 10-cm) POTPIES** ◆

1 recipe Magpie Dough for Flaky Piecrust (page 17), chilled overnight

2 tablespoons unsalted butter

1 medium yellow onion, chopped

3 leeks, halved lengthwise, sliced ½ inch thick, and rinsed in several changes of cold water to remove grit

Kosher salt

2 garlic cloves, minced

2 teaspoons minced fresh thyme leaves

3 tablespoons all-purpose flour

3 cups / 710 ml ham stock or chicken stock

1½ teaspoons dried Dijon mustard

1 tablespoon whole-grain mustard

12 ounces / 340 g cooked ham, cut into ½-inch cubes

2 large Yukon gold potatoes, peeled, cut into ½-inch cubes, and cooked in boiling salted water until tender

4 ounces / 113 g frozen petite peas

1 teaspoon white wine vinegar

Freshly ground black pepper

Butter Parmesan Breadcrumbs (page 210)

Roll, pan, and bake the shells as instructed on pages 36–37. Set the baking sheet on a wire rack and let the shells cool to room temperature while you make the filling.

Melt the butter in a large pot over medium-high heat and sauté the onions and leeks with a pinch of salt. Cover, lower the heat to medium, and cook 10 to 15 minutes or until soft. Stir in the garlic and thyme.

Raise the heat to medium-high. Sprinkle in the flour and cook, stirring constantly, for 1 minute. Whisk in the stock until smooth and thick, about 5 minutes. Stir in the dry and jarred mustards and the ham, potatoes, and peas. Simmer the mixture for 5 to 10 minutes, or until the potatoes are tender. Take the pan off the heat, stir in the vinegar, and season with salt and pepper to taste.

(Continued)

209

Preheat the broiler to high and line a baking sheet with parchment paper. Carefully unmold the potpie shells and set them on the baking sheet. Divide the filling among the shells and top with the butter Parmesan breadcrumbs. Slide the baking sheet under the broiler for 1 to 2 minutes, or just until the crumbs are golden brown. Serve the potpies immediately.

butter parmesan breadcrumbs

This crumb is reminiscent of garlic bread.

MAKES 2 CUPS

4 tablespoons / 56 g unsalted butter, melted

2 cups / 120 g fresh breadcrumbs (page 211)

1 teaspoon granulated garlic

1 teaspoon chopped fresh parsley leaves

½ cup / 56 g grated Parmesan cheese

Kosher salt

Freshly ground black pepper

Melt the butter in a medium skillet over medium heat. Add the breadcrumbs and the granulated garlic and cook, stirring constantly, just until the breadcrumbs are toasted to a light golden color, 2 to 4 minutes. Transfer to a bowl to cool to room temperature.

Stir the parsley and Parmesan into the cooled breadcrumbs and season to taste with salt and pepper.

FRESH BREADCRUMBS

The term "fresh breadcrumbs" is a bit deceptive—it doesn't mean crumbs made from fresh bread, but rather breadcrumbs that aren't packaged. So make your breadcrumbs at home and be sure to use bread that's dry—not stale, and not fresh (the moisture in fresh bread makes for gummy crumbs).

◄ MAKES 3 TO 4 CUPS ►

4 ounces / 113 g sliced, slightly stale country white or Italian bakery bread (10 to 12 slices)

Preheat the oven to 300°F (150°C).

Tear or chop the bread into small pieces (remove the crust if the bread is dense).

Lay the pieces of bread on a baking sheet and dry them out in the oven, just until they're slightly crusty at the edges, 10 to 15 minutes. Halfway through, toss them so they dry evenly.

Fill the bowl of your food processor no more than halfway with the bread pieces and pulse to coarse crumbs.

Store in an airtight container or heavy-duty zip-top bag in the freezer; thaw before using.

macaroni and cheese potpies

Mac and cheese in a pie? Hell yes! This is a perennial Magpie bestseller, whether topped with Old Bay Cheez-It Crunch (page 214) or BBQ Pulled Pork (see Spin, page 214).

◆ **MAKES 8 (4-inch / 10-cm) POTPIES** ◆

1 recipe Magpie Dough for Flaky Piecrust (page 17), chilled overnight

2 cups / 226 g elbow macaroni

4 tablespoons / 56 g unsalted butter, cut into pieces

2 large eggs

1 (12-ounce / 340-ml) can evaporated milk

½ teaspoon hot sauce

1 teaspoon kosher salt

¼ teaspoon freshly ground black pepper

¾ teaspoon dry mustard

3 cups / 340 g grated sharp Cheddar cheese

Old Bay Cheez-It Crunch (page 214)

Follow the instructions on pages 36–37 to roll, pan, and bake the potpie shells. Set the baking sheet on a wire rack and let the shells cool to room temperature while you make the filling.

To make the filling, bring a large pot of salted water to a boil and follow the package instructions to cook the macaroni al dente. Drain the macaroni, return it to the pot, and stir in the butter over medium-low heat. Continue stirring to melt the butter and coat the pasta.

Whisk together the eggs, evaporated milk, hot sauce, salt, pepper, and dry mustard in a mixing bowl.

(Continued)

spin

Mac and Cheese Potpie with BBQ Pulled Pork: *Instead of Cheez-It Crunch, top the potpies with spicy BBQ pulled pork (page 234)—a perfect complement to the creamy, cheesy macaroni.*

Stir the milk mixture into the pot of buttered pasta. Add the cheese and set the pot on the stove over medium-low heat. Stir the mixture constantly for 3 minutes or until creamy.

To assemble the potpies, preheat the oven to 350°F (175°C) with a rack in the center.

Carefully unmold the potpie shells, set them on a baking sheet, and rewarm for 5 to 7 minutes. Divide the mac and cheese among the warm shells, top with Cheez-It crunch, and serve immediately.

old bay cheez-it crunch

Some people top their macaroni and cheese with toasted breadcrumbs, crushed potato chips, Ritz crackers, or even corn flakes. At Magpie, we thought crushed Cheez-Its made sense, so we gave that a try and sprinkled the mixture with Old Bay seasoning to add a bit of spice. Bingo!

MAKES 2 CUPS (ENOUGH TO COVER 8 POTPIES)

4 ounces / 113 g Cheez-It crackers

2 tablespoons unsalted butter, melted

1½ teaspoons Old Bay seasoning

Preheat the oven to 275°F (135°C) with a rack in the center. Line a rimmed baking sheet with parchment paper.

Lightly crush the crackers in a mixing bowl. Add the melted butter and toss to coat. Sprinkle in the Old Bay and continue tossing until the crackers are evenly coated with the spices. Spread the mixture on the lined baking sheet and bake for 6 to 8 minutes, just until lightly toasted. Let the crunch cool before using as topping.

smoked gouda butternut squash pie

This pie makes a perfect vegetarian meal for a cool fall evening or midday brunch.

MAKES 1 (9-inch / 23-cm) PIE

½ recipe Magpie Dough for Flaky Piecrust (page 17), chilled overnight

1 medium (2-pound) butternut squash, peeled, seeded, and cut into ¼-inch-thick slices

1 medium Granny Smith apple, peeled, cored, and sliced ⅛ inch thick

Kosher salt

Freshly ground black pepper

1 tablespoon unsalted butter

1 small yellow onion, diced

2 garlic cloves, minced

2 teaspoons chopped fresh rosemary leaves

½ teaspoon ground or freshly grated nutmeg

1 tablespoon all-purpose flour

1 cup / 237 ml low-sodium chicken stock or water

2 cups / 226 g grated smoked Gouda cheese

4 ounces / 113 g fresh baby spinach

Parmesan Walnut Breadcrumb (page 216)

Roll, pan, and flute the dough as directed on pages 20–23, then follow the directions on page 24 to parbake the crust. Set the pan on a wire rack and let the shell cool to room temperature.

Preheat the oven to 350°F (175°C). Line a rimmed baking sheet with parchment paper.

To make the filling, combine the butternut squash and apples in a large bowl and season with salt and pepper, tossing to mix.

Melt the butter in a large saucepan over medium heat. Add the onions and sauté until translucent. Add the garlic, rosemary, and nutmeg and cook for 1 minute. Whisk in the flour and continue cooking, whisk-

(Continued)

ing constantly, for 1 minute. Add the stock and whisk constantly until the mixture thickens, 5 to 7 minutes. Whisk in ½ cup of the Gouda cheese until melted. Continue whisking in the Gouda ½ cup at a time, melting before each addition. Season the sauce to taste with salt and pepper.

Pour the cheese sauce over the squash mixture and stir to coat completely.

To assemble the pie, set the parbaked pie shell on the parchment-lined baking sheet. Spread half the squash mixture evenly across the bottom of the pie shell. Top with the spinach, followed by the remaining squash mixture. Smooth the top and evenly layer on the parmesan walnut breadcrumb.

Transfer the baking sheet to the oven and bake the pie 45 minutes to 1 hour, or until the squash is tender (the tip of a knife inserted meets no resistance).

parmesan walnut breadcrumbs

You can omit the walnuts, but they give the topping a nice crunch. We created this crumb for the Smoked Gouda Butternut Squash Pie (page 215) but have found that it also makes a delicious alternative topping for Macaroni and Cheese Potpies (page 213).

◆ **MAKES 1 CUP** ◆

1 cup / 80 g fresh breadcrumbs (page 211)

2 tablespoons grated Parmesan cheese

3 tablespoons chopped walnuts (optional)

3 tablespoons unsalted butter, melted

Kosher salt

Freshly ground black pepper

Combine the breadcrumbs, Parmesan, walnuts, and melted butter in a medium bowl, stirring to mix. Season to taste with salt and pepper.

cheeseburger pie

People love a good burger, so when we came up with this pie we suspected it would be a hit with customers. We were so right. In the course of recipe testing for this book, we found that it's a fantastic dish for parties and potlucks—as long as you're serving up enough to meet popular demand (the recipe doubles easily).

◆ MAKES 1 (9-inch / 23-cm) PIE ◆

½ recipe Magpie Dough for Flaky Piecrust (page 17), chilled overnight

1½ pounds / 680 g ground beef

1 small yellow onion, chopped

2 teaspoons steak seasoning spice mix

¼ cup / 20 g fresh breadcrumbs (page 211)

Kosher salt

Freshly ground black pepper

2 large eggs

2 tablespoons ketchup

2 tablespoons yellow mustard

3 tablespoons Worcestershire sauce

2 tablespoons chopped hamburger pickles, plus more whole slices for topping

1½ cups / 170 g grated Cheddar-American cheese blend, divided

Shredded iceberg lettuce, for topping

Sliced plum tomatoes, for topping

Roll, pan, and flute the dough as directed on pages 20–23, then follow the instructions on page 24 to parbake the crust. Set the pan on a wire rack and let the shell cool to room temperature while you make the filling.

Preheat the oven to 350°F (175°C) with a rack in the center. Line a baking sheet with parchment paper.

Brown the ground beef and onions in a large skillet over medium heat. Drain off any drippings, then stir in the steak seasoning and breadcrumbs. Remove the pan from the heat, season with salt and pepper, and set aside to cool slightly.

In a medium bowl, whisk together the eggs, ketchup, mustard, and Worcestershire sauce. Stir in the chopped pickles, then pour the mixture into the cooled ground beef and mix to incorporate. Stir in two-thirds of the cheese.

Set the parbaked piecrust on the lined baking sheet. Pour the cheeseburger mixture into the pie shell, spreading evenly, and bake 30 minutes, rotating halfway through the baking time. Top the pie with the remaining cheese and bake 5 minutes longer, or until the cheese is melted. Let cool for 5 minutes before slicing and serving, each slice topped with shredded lettuce, sliced tomatoes, and pickles.

Bacon Cheeseburger Pie: Add a few strips chopped cooked bacon to the beef filling.

Taco Pie: Use 1 tablespoon of taco seasoning instead of steak seasoning and top each slice with shredded lettuce, salsa, guacamole, and sour cream.

ham loaf pie

The simple country food I grew up on back home was often made out of leftovers of some sort. My Great-Aunt Robie's ham loaf, for one, inevitably showed up on the table soon after Easter. And really, what better way to use up all that ham than by mixing it with some pork sausage, throwing it in a loaf pan, and baking it in the oven? Well, I got to thinking I ought to try reworking Great-Aunt Robie's recipe as a pie, like the meat pies favored by the British (which, back in the day, also typically arose from leftovers). Can't say I was surprised to find it makes a terrific, super-savory pie. Take it in a somewhat different, more holiday ham-flavored direction with Great-Aunt Robie's brown sugar glaze (see Spin, page 221).

◆ **MAKES 1 (9-inch / 23-cm) PIE** ◆

1 recipe Magpie Dough for Flaky Piecrust (page 17), chilled overnight

12 ounces / 340 g loose breakfast or country sausage

12 ounces / 340 g cooked ham, finely ground in a meat grinder or food processor

1 small yellow onion, diced

1 small green bell pepper, diced

¼ cup saltine cracker crumbs

1 large egg, lightly beaten

¾ cup / 177 ml whole milk

Kosher salt

¼ teaspoon freshly ground black pepper

1 large egg yolk

Follow the instructions on page 27 to roll and pan the bottom crust and the sheet of dough for the top crust. Transfer the pan and the baking sheet to the refrigerator to chill the dough while you make the filling.

Preheat the oven to 400°F (200°C) with a rack in the center. Line a rimmed baking sheet with parchment paper.

Brown the sausage in a large skillet over medium heat until cooked through. Use a slotted spoon to transfer the cooked sausage to a large bowl.

Add the ham, onions, and green pepper to the skillet and cook, stirring occasionally, until the vegetables are tender, about 10 minutes.

Stir the vegetable mixture into the bowl with the sausage. Stir in the cracker crumbs, the egg, and the milk. Season the mixture with salt and pepper.

Retrieve the bottom crust from the refrigerator and set the pan on the parchment-lined baking sheet. Spread the filling evenly in the shell. Fetch the sheet of dough for the top crust from the refrigerator and follow the instructions on pages 27–28 to cut decorative vent holes or slits, transfer the top crust onto the pie, and trim and crimp or flute the edges.

Whisk the egg yolk with 1 tablespoon water and lightly brush the top of the pie with the egg wash.

Transfer the baking sheet to the oven and bake the pie 25 minutes, then rotate the baking sheet, reduce the oven temperature to 350°F (175°C), and bake another 15 to 20 minutes, or until the crust is golden. Let cool 10 minutes before slicing and serving.

Glazed Ham Loaf Pie: Whisk together ½ cup (96 g) packed light brown sugar, 2 tablespoons yellow mustard, and ⅛ teaspoon ground clove in a small saucepan over medium-low heat and cook, whisking constantly until the sugar melts and the mixture forms a syrupy glaze. Drizzle the glaze over the finished pie or serve in a pitcher alongside.

shepherd's potpies with cauliflower mash

The usual shepherd's pie is a large casserole-type situation blanketed with mashed potato. At Magpie, we reworked the idea into an individual portion topped with cauliflower mash, which is comfortingly creamy and rich but less bulky than potato—and it adds a serving of vegetables to the picture as well.

MAKES 8 (4-inch / 10-cm) POTPIES

1 recipe Magpie Dough for Flaky Piecrust (page 17), chilled overnight

1½ pounds ground beef

2 tablespoons unsalted butter

1 medium yellow onion, chopped

2 celery stalks, chopped

2 carrots, sliced ¼ inch thick

2 garlic cloves, minced

¼ cup dry sherry

2 tablespoons all-purpose flour

2 cups / 473 ml low-sodium beef stock

1 tablespoon Worcestershire sauce

1 teaspoon chopped fresh thyme leaves

1 cup / 250 g frozen petite peas

1 tablespoon chopped fresh parsley leaves

1 teaspoon kosher salt

½ teaspoon freshly ground black pepper

Cauliflower Mash (page 225)

French's Fried Onions, for serving

Follow the instructions on pages 36–37 to roll, pan, and bake the potpie shells. Set the baking sheet on a wire rack and let the shells cool to room temperature while you make the filling.

Brown the ground beef in a large saucepan over medium-high heat, stirring to crumble, until it is cooked through. Drain off the rendered fat and set the meat aside.

Return the saucepan to the stove and melt the butter over medium heat. Add the onions, celery, and carrots and sauté until they begin to take on a golden color. Add the garlic and cook 1 minute, just until

(Continued)

223

fragrant. Add the sherry and cook until evaporated, stirring to scrape up the tasty brown bits from the bottom of the pan. Add the flour and stir well to coat the vegetables. Continue cooking, stirring constantly, for 1 more minute. Whisk in the beef stock, Worcestershire sauce, and thyme. Bring to a boil, then lower the heat to low, add the cooked beef and the peas, and simmer 10 to 12 minutes, or until the vegetables are tender and the sauce has thickened.

Take the pan off of the heat and stir in the parsley, salt, and pepper. (At this point the filling can be cooled, transferred to airtight containers, and refrigerated for up to 1 week or frozen for up to 1 month. Thaw in the refrigerator overnight; gently rewarm in the microwave or in a saucepan on the stovetop.)

To assemble the potpies, preheat the oven to 350°F (175°C) with a rack in the center. Carefully unmold the potpie shells, set them on a baking sheet, and rewarm in the oven for 5 to 7 minutes. Divide the hot filling among the warm shells, top with hot cauliflower mash, sprinkle with some of the fried onions, and serve.

cauliflower mash

Puréeing in two batches rather than all at once makes it easier to get the mash silky smooth. The mash can be made ahead, cooled, and transferred to airtight containers, then refrigerated for up to 3 days or frozen up to 1 month. Reheat gently.

◁ MAKES 6 CUPS (ENOUGH FOR 8 POTPIES) ▷

1 medium head cauliflower, cut into florets

3 ounces / 85 g cream cheese, cubed, divided

2 ounces / 57 g unsalted butter, cubed, divided

Kosher salt

Freshly ground black pepper

Bring a large pot of salted water to a boil. Add the florets and cook until tender, 7 to 10 minutes. Drain well.

Transfer half of the hot cauliflower florets to the bowl of a food processor fitted with a standard blade. Add half of the cream cheese, half of the butter, and a big pinch of kosher salt and freshly ground pepper. Purée until completely smooth, 2 to 3 minutes, stopping to scrape down the sides a few times. Add the remaining cauliflower, cream cheese, and butter and purée another minute, or until completely smooth. Taste to see if any additional salt and pepper are needed.

Keep warm or reheat gently before topping the potpies.

savory beef potpies

Here's a Sunday supper classic all tucked into a flaky potpie shell. This quick version keeps the vegetables' tender texture and bright color.

MAKES 8 (4-inch / 10-cm) POTPIES

1 recipe Magpie Dough for Flaky Piecrust (page 17), chilled overnight

2 tablespoons unsalted butter

1 pound / 453 g boneless beef sirloin, cut into ½-inch pieces

1 medium yellow onion, chopped

4 celery stalks, chopped

2 medium carrots, sliced ¼ inch thick

1 medium turnip, peeled and cut into ½-inch cubes

1 teaspoon granulated garlic

¼ teaspoon ground allspice

1 teaspoon chopped fresh rosemary leaves

1 teaspoon chopped fresh thyme leaves

1 tablespoon tomato paste

6 tablespoons / 48 g all-purpose flour

3 cups / 710 ml low-sodium beef stock

2 beef bouillon cubes

1 cup / 250 g frozen petite peas

1 teaspoon minced fresh parsley

Kosher salt

Freshly ground black pepper

8 slices French baguette, toasted and buttered

Follow the instructions on pages 36–37 to roll, pan, and bake the potpie shells. Set the baking sheet on a wire rack and let the shells cool to room temperature while you make the filling.

In a large heavy pot or Dutch oven, melt the butter over medium-high heat and add half the beef. Brown the meat on all sides, then use a slotted spoon to transfer it to a bowl. Repeat with the remaining beef.

Add the onions, celery, carrots, and turnip to the beef drippings in the pan. Cook over medium heat, stirring occasionally, until the vegetables are tender, 5 to 10 minutes. Stir in the granulated garlic, allspice, rosemary, thyme, and tomato paste and cook, stirring constantly, until fragrant, about 30 seconds.

Put the flour in a bowl and whisk in the beef stock until the flour dissolves.

Raise the heat under the vegetables to medium-high and whisk in the flour slurry. Continue cooking, whisking constantly, until the liquid starts to thicken to a gravy consistency, then bring it to a boil and cook for 1 more minute.

Stir in the bouillon cubes and the browned beef. Simmer for 10 to 15 minutes, stirring occasionally. Stir in the peas and the parsley and simmer 5 minutes. Season the stew to taste with salt and pepper.

To assemble the potpies, preheat the oven to 350°F (175°C) with a rack in the center. Carefully unmold the potpie shells, set them on a baking sheet, and rewarm in the oven for 5 to 7 minutes. Divide the hot filling among the 8 potpie shells and top with toasted baguette.

SAVORY HAND PIES

Raid your refrigerator for savory leftovers—sauce, stew, chowder, just about anything sautéed, braised, or roasted. Be sure not to overlook the deli drawer—pepperoni, salami, sliced ham and turkey, and any and all manner of cheese are fantastic fodder for hand pies. Ditto condiments—from seedy mustard to sauerkraut, salsa to chutney, roasted peppers to olive tapenade, and so forth.

Combine a dab of this, a morsel of that, enfolding up to about 2 tablespoons total in each 4-inch dough circle (page 40). Brush the edges with a little egg wash and crimp to seal. Brush the tops with egg wash and sprinkle with a little coarse sea salt. Set the hand pies on a parchment-lined baking sheet, chill for 15 minutes while you preheat the oven to 375°F (190°C), then slide them into the oven and bake 20 to 25 minutes, or until golden.

Cool 10 minutes on a wire rack. Call them hors d'oeuvres, empanadas, hot pockets, breakfast, lunch, dinner, late-night snack, whatever's most apt and appetizing—and enjoy!

spaghetti herb pie

A healthy helping of marinara on top is essential to the pleasure of this perfect pasta pie—its acidity and flavor make it a bright, tangy counterpoint to the rich filling, which is creamy with mozzarella, fragrant with fresh herbs and lemon zest, studded with little pockets of ricotta and green peas, and topped with crisp Parmesan crumb.

⟨ MAKES 1 (9-inch / 23-cm) PIE ⟩

½ recipe Magpie Dough for Flaky Piecrust (page 17), chilled overnight

1 (12-ounce / 340-ml) can evaporated milk

2 large eggs

½ teaspoon kosher salt

1 teaspoon granulated garlic

1 teaspoon granulated onion

¼ teaspoon red pepper flakes

⅛ teaspoon freshly ground black pepper, plus more as needed

8 ounces / 227 g spaghetti

2½ cups / 284 g grated whole-milk mozzarella cheese

1 tablespoon minced fresh parsley leaves

2 tablespoons minced fresh basil leaves

2 tablespoons minced fresh chives

½ teaspoon freshly grated lemon zest

⅓ cup / 83 g whole-milk ricotta cheese

⅓ cup / 50 g frozen petite peas

¼ cup / 25 g grated Parmesan cheese, divided

1 cup / 80 g fresh breadcrumbs (page 211), toasted

Kosher salt

About 2 cups / 514 g homemade or good-quality jarred marinara sauce, for serving

Roll, pan, and flute the dough as directed on pages 20–23, then follow the instructions on page 24 to parbake the crust. Set the pan on a wire rack and let cool to room temperature while you make the filling.

Preheat the oven to 375°F (190°C) with a rack in the center.

Whisk the evaporated milk, eggs, salt, granulated garlic and onion, red pepper flakes, and black pepper together in a medium bowl.

Bring a large pot of salted water to a boil and follow the package instructions to cook the pasta al dente, then drain and return it to the pot.

Pour the milk mixture into the pot of hot spaghetti, add half of the mozzarella, and cook a few minutes over medium heat, stirring constantly, just until the cheese is melted. Add the remaining mozzarella and continue to cook, stirring constantly, until the cheese is melted and the liquid begins to thicken. Take the pan off the heat.

Toss the herbs together in a small bowl. Measure out and reserve 1 tablespoon of the herbs for topping the pie; stir the remaining herbs and the lemon zest into the pasta.

Set the cooled piecrust on the parchment-lined baking sheet. Use a pasta server or a pair of tongs to transfer half of the spaghetti mixture into the shell. Spread the pasta evenly, dot with the ricotta and peas, and sprinkle with 2 tablespoons of the Parmesan. Top with the remaining spaghetti, followed by the toasted breadcrumbs, the remaining 2 tablespoons Parmesan, and the reserved herbs. Lightly season the top of the pie with kosher salt and black pepper.

Slide the baking sheet into the oven and bake the pie 25 to 30 minutes, or until set (no longer jiggly in the center), rotating halfway through the baking time.

Set the pan on a wire rack and let the pie cool 10 minutes before slicing and serving, with ¼ cup warm marinara on top or alongside each slice.

< MAGPIE >

chicken biscuit potpies

When it comes to comfort food, nothing beats a homemade chicken potpie. Ours is topped with a lovely Cheddar biscuit (page 232). Note that all three components (shell, filling, biscuit) freeze beautifully, so this is a great make-ahead for weeknights or whenever.

◆ MAKES 8 (4-inch / 10-cm) POTPIES ◆

1 recipe Magpie Dough for Flaky Piecrust (page 17), chilled overnight

2 tablespoons unsalted butter

1 medium yellow onion, chopped

4 celery stalks, chopped

2 medium carrots, sliced ¼ inch thick

6 tablespoons / 48 g all-purpose flour

3 cups / 710 ml low-sodium chicken stock

1 teaspoon granulated garlic

1 teaspoon poultry seasoning

2 cubes chicken bouillon

1 pound / 453 g boneless, skinless chicken thighs, cut into ½-inch pieces

1 cup / 250 g fresh or frozen petite peas

2 teaspoons minced fresh chives

2 teaspoons minced fresh parsley leaves

½ teaspoon freshly squeezed lemon juice

Kosher salt

Freshly ground black pepper

Cheddar Biscuits (page 232)

Follow the instructions on pages 36–37 to roll, pan, and bake the potpie shells. Set the baking sheet on a wire rack and let the shells cool while you make the filling.

Melt the butter in a large pot or Dutch oven over medium heat and sauté the onions, celery, and carrots until tender, 5 to 10 minutes.

Meanwhile, put the flour in a large mixing bowl and whisk in the chicken stock until the flour is completely dissolved.

Add the garlic granules and poultry seasoning to the vegetables in the pot and cook 30 seconds, just until fragrant. Raise the heat to medium-high and whisk in the flour slurry. Continue whisking as the gravy starts to thicken and

(Continued)

comes to a boil, then continue whisking and cooking for 1 minute more. Stir in the bouillon, chicken pieces, and peas and simmer the mixture 10 to 15 minutes, or until the chicken is cooked through, stirring occasionally. Stir in the chives, parsley, and lemon juice. Season to taste with salt and pepper. (At this point the filling can be cooled, transferred to airtight containers, and kept in the refrigerator for up to 3 days or frozen up to 1 month. Thaw in the refrigerator overnight; gently rewarm in the microwave or in a saucepan on the stovetop.)

To assemble the potpies, preheat the oven to 350°F (175°C). Carefully unmold the potpie shells, set them on a baking sheet, and rewarm in the oven for 5 to 7 minutes. Divide the hot filling among the warm potpie shells. Top each potpie with a warm Cheddar biscuit and serve immediately.

cheddar biscuits

This recipe is very easy and very rewarding. Just be sure to follow the mixing instructions closely so you get light, airy, tender biscuits. Flecks of parsley make the golden biscuits even prettier; note that it's important to use dried rather than fresh, which would tint the dough an off color.

◆ MAKES 8 LARGE BISCUITS ◆

2 cups / 280 g all-purpose flour

2 teaspoons baking powder

½ teaspoon baking soda

2 tablespoons granulated sugar

1 teaspoon fine salt

¼ teaspoon freshly ground black pepper, plus more for topping

½ teaspoon granulated garlic

¼ teaspoon red pepper flakes

1 teaspoon dried parsley flakes, plus more for topping

1 cup / 113 g grated sharp Cheddar cheese

1 cup / 237 ml cold whole milk

10 tablespoons /142 g unsalted butter, melted and cooled slightly, divided

Flaky sea salt (we use Maldon at the shop), for topping

Preheat the oven to 425°F (220°C) with a rack in the center. Line a large baking sheet with parchment paper.

In a mixing bowl, whisk together the flour, baking powder, baking soda, sugar, salt, and spices. Add the cheese and toss to coat and separate the shreds.

Combine the milk and 8 tablespoons of the melted butter in a medium bowl, using a fork to stir until the butter forms small clumps.

Add the milk mixture to the flour mixture and stir just until the ingredients are incorporated and the batter pulls away from the sides of the bowl. Using a large spoon, scoop and drop eight biscuits onto the prepared baking sheet. Brush the tops of the biscuits with remaining 2 tablespoons of melted butter and sprinkle with sea salt, black pepper, and parsley flakes.

Bake the biscuits until the tops are golden brown and crisp, about 12 minutes. Store in an airtight container for up to 2 days or freeze for up to 1 month (to defrost, wrap in foil and warm in a low oven).

pulled pork potpies with coleslaw

Use homemade barbecue sauce or your favorite store-bought one; at the shop we use Bull's-Eye Original as a base and add additional spices to it. Note that the rubbed pork needs to be marinated for eight to 24 hours, then slow-cooked for up to a full day, so make sure you plan ahead. A dill pickle on the side brings a nice contrast to the rich pork.

MAKES 8 (4-inch / 10-cm) POTPIES

3 tablespoons packed light brown sugar

¼ cup / 8 g smoked sweet paprika

2 teaspoons granulated garlic

2 teaspoons granulated onion

2 teaspoons chili powder

2 teaspoons kosher salt

1 (5-pound) boneless pork butt roast, trimmed and cut into 4-inch pieces

2 cups / 473 ml low-sodium chicken stock

1 recipe Magpie Dough for Flaky Piecrust (page 17), chilled overnight

1½ cups / 355 ml barbecue sauce

Coleslaw (page 235), for topping

Petite dill pickles, for serving

Whisk together the dry ingredients in a small bowl. Rub the mixture all over the pieces of pork. Put the pork in a heavy-duty zip-top bag and chill in the refrigerator for 8 to 24 hours.

Transfer the marinated pork to a slow cooker. Pour the stock over the meat, cover, and cook until the pork is fork-tender (stick a fork into the meat and try to rotate it 90 degrees, if it twists easily and seems to shred, it's done), 9 to 11 hours on low or 5 to 7 hours on high.

While the pork cooks, follow the instructions on pages 36–37 to roll, pan, and bake the potpie shells. Set the baking sheet on a wire rack and let the shells cool to room temperature while you finish preparing the pulled pork.

Transfer the pork to a large bowl and let it cool slightly. Pour the liquid from the slow cooker through a strainer and set aside separately. Shred the pork, discarding skin and excess fat. Return the shredded pork to the slow cooker. If need be, skim and discard fat from the surface of the strained liquid. Add the reserved strained cooking liquid to the pork, ¼ cup at a time, until moistened as desired. Add the barbecue sauce and toss to coat the pork evenly. Reheat the pulled pork filling.

To assemble the potpies, preheat the oven to 350°F (175°C) with a rack in the center. Carefully unmold the potpie shells, set them on a baking sheet, and bake for 5 to 7 minutes to rewarm. Divide the hot filling among the 8 warm potpie shells, top with slaw, and serve with a petite pickle.

coleslaw

Our coleslaw is more savory than sweet, to help balance the smoky sweet barbecue sauce.

MAKES 3 TO 4 CUPS

½ cup / 85 g mayonnaise

1 teaspoon celery seed

2 tablespoons freshly squeezed lemon juice

1 teaspoon granulated sugar

½ teaspoon mustard

1 teaspoon minced fresh scallions (white and green parts)

4 cups / 400 g shredded green cabbage (1 small head)

1 teaspoon fine salt

Freshly ground black pepper

Combine the mayo, celery seed, lemon juice, sugar, mustard, and scallions in a large mixing bowl and whisk to blend. Add the cabbage and stir well to coat. Add the salt and mix well. Season to taste with additional salt and freshly ground black pepper.

mole chili frito potpies

This recipe makes a lot of chili—enough to fill at least 8 potpies, plus more to enjoy as leftovers. It's easy and delicious to use up by the bowlful with various toppings or spread on nachos. Or freeze the chili for another round of potpies at a later date (yet another good reason to keep a batch of potpie shells on hand in the freezer). To make the recipe vegetarian-friendly, just omit the chorizo.

MAKES 8 (4-inch / 10-cm) POTPIES

1 recipe Magpie Dough for Flaky Piecrust (page 17), chilled overnight

2 tablespoons vegetable oil

3 links Spanish chorizo, cut into ¼-inch dice

1 large yellow onion, chopped

1 large green bell pepper, chopped

1 large red bell pepper, chopped

5 garlic cloves, minced

1 teaspoon chipotle chili powder

1 tablespoon ground cumin

1 tablespoon dried oregano

¼ teaspoon ground cinnamon

1 teaspoon hot smoked paprika

¾ teaspoon kosher salt, plus more for seasoning

½ teaspoon freshly ground black pepper, plus more for seasoning

2 (15-ounce) cans black beans, rinsed and drained

1 (15-ounce) can garbanzo beans, rinsed and drained

3 (14-ounce) cans whole tomatoes, chopped, with liquid

1 cup frozen yellow corn

2 ounces semisweet chocolate, chopped

1 (9.75-ounce / 276 g) bag Fritos or tortilla chips

2 cups / 226 g grated Monterey Jack and/or sharp Cheddar cheese

Sour cream, sliced avocados, thinly sliced radishes, thinly sliced scallions (white and green parts), pickled jalapeño slices, for topping

Follow the instructions on pages 36–37 to roll, pan, and bake the potpie shells. Set the baking sheet on a wire rack and let the shells cool to room temperature while you make the filling.

To make the mole chili, heat the oil in a large pot or Dutch oven over medium-high heat. Add the chorizo and cook until the sausage starts to release its juices, about 5 minutes. Add the onions and peppers and sauté until the vegetables are tender and caramelizing nicely at the edges, 5 to 7 minutes. Lower the heat to medium-low, add the garlic, and cook 1 minute, then stir in the spices and the salt and pepper and cook for about 3 minutes, just until fragrant. Stir in

(Continued)

the beans and tomatoes and turn the heat back up to medium-high to bring the chili to a boil, then reduce to a simmer, cover, and cook for 30 minutes, stirring occasionally. Add the corn and cook the chili for another 5 minutes.

Remove the pot from the heat, stir in the chocolate and additional salt and pepper to taste. (At this point the chili can be cooled, transferred to airtight containers, and refrigerated for up to 3 days or frozen for up to 1 month. Thaw in the refrigerator overnight; gently rewarm in the micro-wave or in a saucepan on the stovetop.)

To assemble and serve the potpies, preheat the broiler to low and line a baking sheet with parchment paper.

Carefully unmold the potpie shells and set them on the parchment-lined baking sheet. Ladle the chili filling into the shells, filling each to the top. Top with Fritos and grated cheese and slide the baking sheet under the broiler for a minute or two, just until the cheese melts and the edges of the chips turn toasty brown.

Top the pies with sour cream, avocado, radishes, scallions, and pickled jalapeños, or serve the toppings in small bowls for everyone to add their own.

thanksgiving potpies

Why do we eat Thanksgiving dinner only once a year? It's one of my favorite holiday meals, so I turned the feast into cozy potpies. Keep some shells, filling, and stuffing in the freezer and you can whip these up in no time, anytime.

MAKES 8 (4-inch / 10-cm) POTPIES

1 recipe Magpie Dough for Flaky Piecrust (page 17), chilled overnight

2 tablespoons unsalted butter

1 medium yellow onion, chopped

4 celery stalks, chopped

2 medium carrots, sliced ¼ inch thick

6 tablespoons / 48 g all-purpose flour

3 cups / 710 ml low-sodium turkey or chicken stock

1 teaspoon granulated garlic

1 teaspoon poultry seasoning

2 teaspoons Better Than Bouillon turkey base

1 pound / 453 g boneless, skinless turkey breast, cut into ½-inch pieces

1 cup / 250 g frozen petite peas

1 cup / 250 g frozen corn

1 teaspoon minced fresh parsley leaves

½ teaspoon freshly squeezed lemon juice

Kosher salt

Freshly ground black pepper

Apple Fennel Stuffing (page 242), for topping

1 (14-ounce / 397-g) can cranberry sauce, for topping

Follow the instructions on pages 36–37 to roll, pan, and bake the potpie shells. Set the baking sheet on a wire rack and let the shells cool to room temperature while you make the filling.

Melt the butter in a large pot or Dutch oven over medium heat and sauté the onions, celery, and carrots until tender, 5 to 10 minutes.

Meanwhile, make the slurry. Put the flour in a bowl and whisk in the stock until the flour dissolves.

When the vegetables are tender, add the garlic granules and poultry seasoning to the pan and cook until fragrant, about 30 seconds. Turn the heat under the pan up to medium-high and whisk in the slurry. Cook, whisking constantly,

(Continued)

until the mixture starts to thicken to a gravy consistency. Then bring the mixture to a boil and cook for 2 minutes, stirring often to prevent the mixture from sticking to the bottom of the pan and scorching.

Stir in the bouillon and the turkey pieces. Lower the heat and simmer, uncovered, for 10 to 15 minutes, or until the turkey is cooked through, stirring often. Add the peas and corn and simmer for another 5 minutes. Take the pan off the heat and stir in the parsley and lemon juice. Season to taste with salt and pepper. (At this point the filling can be cooled, transferred to airtight containers, and refrigerated for up to 3 days or frozen for up to 1 month. Thaw in the refrigerator overnight; gently rewarm in the microwave or in a saucepan on the stovetop.)

To assemble the potpies, preheat the broiler to low. Line a baking sheet with parchment paper.

Carefully unmold the potpie shells and set them on the lined baking sheet. Divide the filling among the shells and top with warm apple fennel stuffing. Slide the baking sheet under the broiler for 2 to 3 minutes, or until the stuffing begins to toast up.

Serve with cranberry sauce, heaped either on top or on the side.

apple fennel stuffing

This is a basic, classic, Thanksgiving 101 stuffing. In other words, it's the perfect topping for a savory turkey potpie.

MAKES ABOUT 5 CUPS; ENOUGH TO TOP 8 (4-inch / 10-cm) **POTPIES**

6 ounces / 170 g Martin's potato bread stuffing (½ bag)

3 tablespoons unsalted butter

1½ teaspoons fennel seed

1 small yellow onion, chopped

2 celery stalks, chopped

1 medium unpeeled Gala, Honeycrisp, or other crisp, sweet apple, cored and cut into ½-inch dice

½ teaspoon plus pinch kosher salt

½ teaspoon poultry seasoning

½ teaspoon granulated garlic

½ teaspoon granulated onion

¼ cup / 59 ml chicken stock

2 teaspoons minced fresh parsley leaves

¼ teaspoon freshly ground black pepper

Put the bread cubes in a medium bowl and set aside.

Melt the butter in a medium saucepan over medium heat. Add the fennel seeds and cook until fragrant, 5 to 7 minutes. Add the onions, celery, apple, and a pinch of salt. Cook until vegetables are tender, 5 to 7 minutes. Stir in the poultry seasoning and the granulated garlic and onion, cooking until fragrant, about 30 seconds. Add the chicken stock and heat until steaming.

Pour the stock mixture over the bread cubes, tossing to coat. Stir in the parsley. Season to taste with the salt and pepper.

The cooled stuffing can be stored in an airtight container in the refrigerator for up to 5 days or in the freezer for up to 1 month. Thaw in the refrigerator overnight; gently rewarm in the microwave or oven.

seafood chowder potpies

These chowder potpies make a great hearty supper just about any time of year. You can use whatever mild white fish you like. The smoky bacon adds a nice touch of richness but can be left out if need be.

◄ ❈ **MAKES 8 (4-inch / 10-cm) POTPIES** ❈ ►

1 recipe Magpie Dough for Flaky Piecrust (page 17), chilled overnight

4 slices bacon, coarsely chopped

2 tablespoons unsalted butter

1 large yellow onion, finely chopped

2 carrots, finely chopped

2 celery stalks, finely chopped

3 tablespoons all-purpose flour

1 teaspoon smoked sweet mild paprika

2 (8-ounce) bottles clam juice

1 cup / 232 g heavy cream

2 large russet potatoes, cut into ¼-inch pieces

1 pound / 453 g skinned cod or haddock fillets, cut into ½-inch pieces

8 ounces / 226 g small shrimp, peeled and deveined

3 tablespoons minced fresh parsley leaves

Kosher salt

Freshly ground black pepper

Chive Crumble (page 245)

Follow the instructions on pages 36–37 to roll, pan, and bake the potpie shells. Set the baking sheet on a wire rack and let the shells cool to room temperature while you make the chowder filling.

Cook the bacon in a large saucepan over medium heat until crisp, 7 to 10 minutes. Remove the bacon from the pan and set it on a paper towel-lined plate to drain.

Drain the bacon fat from the pan, set the pan over medium heat, and add the butter, onions, carrot, and celery, sautéing until the vegetables have softened, 5 to 7 minutes.

Sprinkle the flour over the vegetables and cook, stirring constantly, for 3 minutes. Add the paprika and continue cooking and stirring

(Continued)

constantly for another 30 seconds. Stir in the clam juice, ½ cup water, and the cream. Raise the heat under the pan to medium-high and bring the chowder to a boil, stirring often to prevent scorching.

When the chowder comes to a boil, stir in the potatoes, lower the heat under the pan to medium, and simmer, uncovered, for 12 minutes. Add the fish and shrimp and simmer until both are cooked (opaque at the center), about 5 minutes. Stir in the parsley and the crispy bacon. Season to taste with salt and pepper. (At this point the chowder can be cooled, transferred to airtight containers, and refrigerated for up to 3 days or frozen for up to 1 month. Thaw in the refrigerator overnight; gently rewarm in the micro-wave or in a saucepan on the stovetop.)

To assemble the potpies, preheat the oven to 350°F (175°C) with a rack in the center. Carefully unmold the potpie shells, set them on a baking sheet, and rewarm in the oven for 5 to 7 minutes. Divide the chowder fill-ing among the warm shells, topping each potpie with about ¼ cup chive crumble. Serve immediately.

chive crumble

These savory crumbles are like oyster crackers, only better. Don't be surprised if you catch yourself snacking on them while you're making the filling.

◆ **MAKES ABOUT 2 CUPS; ENOUGH TO TOP 8 (4-inch / 10-cm) POTPIES** ◆

2¼ cups / 283 g all-purpose flour

2 teaspoons baking powder

¾ teaspoon fine salt

½ teaspoon freshly ground black pepper

⅛ teaspoon cayenne pepper

1 teaspoon granulated garlic

6 tablespoons / 85 g cold unsalted butter, cut into ½-inch cubes

1 tablespoon chopped fresh chives

1 ounce / 28 g Parmesan cheese, cut into ½-inch pieces

¾ cup / 170 g heavy cream

Preheat the oven to 375°F (190°C) with a rack in the center. Line a rimmed baking sheet with parchment paper.

Combine the flour, baking powder, salt, black pepper, cayenne, and granulated garlic in the bowl of a food processor. Pulse the machine 5 times, then scatter the butter pieces over the flour mixture and pulse 5 more times, or until the mixture resembles coarse cornmeal. Add the chives and Parmesan and pulse 3 to 5 times to incorporate. Pour in the heavy cream and continue pulsing the machine until the mixture gathers together into an irregular mass.

Crumble the mixture into an even layer on the prepared baking sheet. Bake 10 to 12 minutes, or until lightly browned. Let the crumble cool completely before topping potpies.

The cooled crumble can be stored in an airtight container at room temperature for up to 5 days or in the freezer for up to 1 month.

chicken corn pie

This hearty pie is partly a play on chicken corn soup, a staple potluck dish back home in central PA, where it's the soup at pretty much every event—from church supper to country fair. This pie also harkens back to my family's recipe for corn casserole, which my grandfather used to make with dried Indian corn soaked overnight in milk. It has evolved into a similar dish made with cream-style corn from a can and kernel corn we've cut off cobs and frozen to use year-round.

MAKES 1 (9-inch / 23-cm) PIE

1 recipe Magpie Dough for Flaky Piecrust (page 17), chilled overnight

1 large Yukon gold potato, peeled and cut into ¼-inch cubes

4 tablespoons / 56 g unsalted butter

1 small yellow onion, finely chopped

2 celery stalks, finely chopped

1 cup / 150 g fresh or frozen sweet corn kernels (ideally cut off cobs in summer and frozen) or
1 (15-ounce / 425-g) can whole corn kernels, drained

1 large egg

1 (14.75-ounce / 418-g) can cream-style corn

½ cup / 120 ml whole milk

1 cup / 125 g shredded cooked chicken

Kosher salt

Freshly ground black pepper

1 large egg yolk

Roll and pan the bottom crust as directed on page 29. Follow the instructions on page 31 to roll and cut the sheet of dough for the top crust into 2-inch-wide strips for a wide lattice top. Set the pan and the baking sheet in the refrigerator to chill while you make the filling.

Preheat the oven to 400°F (200°C) with a rack in the center. Line a baking sheet with parchment paper.

Bring 3 cups salted water to a boil in a small pot. Add the potatoes and cook until tender, 3 to 5 minutes. Drain and set aside.

Melt the butter in a medium sauté pan over medium heat and cook the onions, celery, and whole corn kernels until tender, 5 to 7 minutes.

Set aside to cool for 10 minutes.

Beat the egg in a large bowl, then whisk in the creamed corn and milk. Fold in the potatoes, corn kernel mixture, and chicken and season with salt and pepper.

Retrieve the bottom crust from the refrigerator and set the pan on the parchment-lined baking sheet. Pour the filling into the shell. Fetch the dough strips from the refrigerator and follow the instructions on page 31 to lattice the top of the pie. Lightly beat the egg yolk with 1 tablespoon water and lightly brush the lattice.

Transfer the baking sheet to the oven and bake the pie 25 minutes, then rotate the sheet, reduce the oven temperature to 350°F (175°C), and bake another 15 to 20 minutes, or until the juices bubble up through the lattice and the crust is golden.

Set the baking sheet on a wire rack and let the pie cool 10 minutes before slicing and serving.

acknowledgments

THANK YOU—

To my extended, multigenerational family—aunts and uncles, grandparents and great-grandparents, for giving me traditions, history, and memories I'll always cherish.

To my hometown, Carlisle, Pennsylvania, for teaching me to slow down and enjoy a slice of pie every now and again.

To my parents and siblings, for listening to all my trials and tribulations while creating the shop and reminding me it would all work out.

To my friends, young and old, for encouraging me every step of the way that having more pie in the world was a worthy mission.

To culinary school, for helping me realize I had a lot more talent in me than just being a designer.

To the Magpie team, past and present, for helping to create a pleasant and memorable experience for all of our customers—and for being the biggest Magpie fans ever.

To 20nine, for developing a brand that captured the Magpie secret ingredient . . . love.

To Jeff Sacks, for offering his photography skills in the beginning and thus helping bring our humble pies to life.

To Sky Strouth, for locating the perfect spot for Magpie and helping to guide me through the arduous process of opening a restaurant.

To Kristen Green Wiewora and the staff at Running Press, for believing there should be more pie in the world and asking me to help spread the good word.

YOU'RE THE BEST—

Chef Tony Horvath, for believing in me, encouraging me, and inspiring me to open a pie shop.

Cynthia Jordan, for your 1 1/2 years of dedication, energy, and hardcore pie baking.

Rebecca Smith, for taking the pie-baking baton and running with it.

Peter Breslow, for great PR and getting the word out that there's something new here in Philly: pie.

Dan May, for writing a song about Magpie being a slice of heaven, I guarantee.

Miriam Harris, for taking what seemed like mundane stories of my childhood and capturing a magic in them—when I read these pages I can smell the honeysuckle on the warm summer air.

index

NOTE: Page references in *italics* indicate photographs.